THIS IS YOUR WAKE UP CALL

DITCH THE SABOTAGE AND REWIRE THE SH*T RUNNING YOUR LIFE

Erin C. Corman, MS

Spark.

For permission requests, write to the publisher at:
Spark Yoga, LLC
sparkyogawellness@gmail.com

ISBN: 979-8-9931792-0-9

Cover design by Erin C. Corman
Interior design by Erin C. Corman

Disclaimer: This book is a work of nonfiction drawing on personal experience, psychological research, and spiritual traditions. It is not intended as a substitute for professional medical, psychological, or legal advice. Readers should seek appropriate licensed professionals where needed.

Trademarks:

All references to Marvel characters, stories, or related properties in this book are used strictly for commentary, metaphor, and educational purposes. They are included as cultural touchstones to help illustrate concepts—not as reproductions of original works.

Marvel and all related character names, images, and properties are trademarks of Marvel Entertainment, LLC. This work is not affiliated with, endorsed by, or sponsored by Marvel Entertainment, LLC or any of its subsidiaries.

In plain terms: Marvel built the superheroes. I just borrowed them as examples to help you see your own superpowers and sabotage patterns more clearly.

Printed in the United States of America

First Edition

To my wonderfully grounded husband &
loving wild child of a daughter.

contents

One

THE WAKE UP CALL

The Moment You Realize You Can't Keep Bullshitting Yourself

I t doesn't always look like a breakdown. Sometimes, it's quieter—more insidious. Sometimes, it's just *Tuesday*.

You're doing the damn dishes. Or staring at an email you've already reread ten times. The kids are screaming in the background. The coffee's cold. Your chest is tight—but not in a dramatic panic-attack way, just a dull pressure that's been building for months. Years, maybe.

You're moving through your days, ticking the boxes, doing what you've always done. From the outside, it looks fine. Maybe even good. But something inside is slowly unraveling. Not with a scream, but with a whisper: *Is this all there is?*

No lightning bolts. No spiritual awakenings under a full moon. Just the quiet, brutal truth: **You've outgrown the life you built.**

It may be the job, the relationship, or even the roles you've been playing so well, for so long.

Suddenly, the routine feels like a fucking trap. And you realize—you've been shrinking. For safety. For others. For the version of yourself that felt manageable and acceptable. But the truth is clawing its way out.

This is the wake-up call.

For many people, particularly women in midlife, this moment comes not with fanfare, but with a slow burn of discontent. You've spent decades building a life, often one centered around expectations—societal, familial, internal. You've climbed ladders, raised families, nurtured everyone else, played by the rules. And then one day you wake up and realize that somewhere along the way, you've lost touch with yourself. Not in a dramatic, cinematic way. But in the quiet ache of disconnection that settles within your bones.

Then, the questioning begins...do you share this with others? Your friends? Your partner? Your therapist? Are you the only one feeling this way...having these thoughts? You decide to talk with your partner—let's say he's a man around your age—more on that later. When you finally get brave enough to voice what's been simmering beneath the surface, he looks at you like you've grown three heads. He tells you you're just hormonal. That it's probably just a phase. Maybe even a midlife crisis. You stare at him in disbelief, wondering if you should laugh or scream. Instead, you smirk and think, "Cool. Thanks, Doc." And just like that, you tuck it away and try to hide your crazy. Cue Miranda Lambert's *Mama's Broken Heart.*

At the very best, you find friends to joke around with about this idea of "life is going nuts" and "I'm stepping into my moon child phase". Everyone seems to understand that it is nothing more than just that...a phase. A moment in your life that you will pick yourself up by the bootstraps and just keep swimming. So many phrases we can insert here.

By joking about this calling, this itch, we are only adding to the already societal comment about what is truly happening within. This is not a freaking midlife crisis. It is not, and let me make this abundantly clear, it is not a mental breakdown. This is a normal part of our life cycle and it is way more than just hormones.

This chapter isn't about breakdowns as failures. It's about understanding them as thresholds. These moments of discomfort, of internal tension, of existential unease—they're not signs that something's wrong with you. They're signals. They're invitations to reassess, realign, and reclaim. They're the first stirrings of a mindshift.

What Leads People to Realize They Need a Change

There is a unique pain in living a life that looks good on paper but feels hollow in the soul. For many, the signs don't always scream, they creep in subtly. You find yourself doom-scrolling, numbing out to Netflix, rage-cleaning, or over-scheduling just to "feel something". You're successful by outside standards—but hollow on the inside. You catch yourself fantasizing about escaping it all, not because you're reckless... but because you're *exhausted* by your own performance. It's in the moments you can't quite name—the irritability that doesn't go away, the fatigue that sleep can't fix, the quiet resentment that bubbles beneath the surface. Over time, it becomes harder to ignore.

Underneath it all? There is a quiet, pulsing "no". A no to the life you're currently living. A no to the roles you never consciously chose. To the watered-down version of you that got stuck on autopilot. Eventually, the discomfort of staying the same outweighs the fear of changing. That's the tipping point.

And it doesn't come all at once. Sometimes it's a slow drip—a little voice getting louder. Sometimes it's a punch in the gut—a betrayal, a layoff, a breakdown that breaks *you* open. But one way or another, you find yourself face-to-face with the truth: **You're not okay living this half-life anymore.**

Often, this recognition begins in the body. As Bessel van der Kolk explores in *The Body Keeps the Score*, the body stores trauma, emotional pain, and suppressed experience in physiological patterns long after the conscious mind has moved on. The nervous system becomes the ledger—recording what the brain can't always process in the moment. You start noticing that your shoulders are constantly tense, your jaw clenched, your breath shallow. These aren't random symptoms; they're the body's language. Subtle, persistent signals that something in your inner or outer environment is no longer in alignment. They are indicators that your body is no longer in harmony with the life you are leading. Going unchecked, these constant stressors and suppressed emotions build to more serious medical conditions—chronic inflammation, autoimmune disorders, cardiovascular disease, gastrointestinal issues, and even cognitive decline.

I know this intimately. For years, I battled with Irritable Bowel Syndrome (IBS)—a condition that no amount of diet changes or medications could truly resolve. Well...that was at least the only thing the doctors would treat me for. I went in for so many tests, saw countless doctors and specialists, racked up tons of medical debt, only to be given a pill and a shoulder shrug. But beneath the frustration was a truth I hadn't been ready to see: this wasn't just a physical issue. My body wasn't malfunctioning—it was trying to talk to me. Every flare-up was a message. A demand to slow down, to listen, to feel what I had spent years suppressing. It wasn't just about what I was eating—it was about what I was holding in.

The body doesn't just whisper when it's overwhelmed; over time, it starts to scream. As Van der Kolk explains, trauma and stress left unresolved can lead to physiological changes in brain structure, immune response, and hormonal regulation. What starts as subtle tension can snowball into a breakdown of the body's ability to regulate and repair itself.

This is particularly relevant when we consider the autonomic nervous system—specifically, the interplay between the sympathetic and parasympathetic branches. The sympathetic nervous system triggers our 'fight or flight' response, meant to protect us in moments of acute danger. But for many people, chronic stress means this system is activated far too often, leaving them in a perpetual state of hypervigilance. Over time, this dysregulation wears down the body, impairing sleep, digestion, immunity, and hormonal balance.

The parasympathetic nervous system—our 'rest and digest' mode—is supposed to counterbalance this, but for those with high stress loads, unresolved trauma, or energetic blockages, access to this state becomes more difficult. The body forgets how to rest. The system forgets how to reset. This is often where we begin to see conditions like Chronic Fatigue Syndrome (CFS) or Adrenal Fatigue Syndrome (AFS) emerge. In many cases, CFS and AFS are not simply a medical anomaly but a physiological response to sustained nervous system dysregulation. The fatigue isn't laziness—it's the result of a system that's been in overdrive for too long without a true recovery cycle.

Later in my journey, I was diagnosed with this very thing. I thought I was fine...okay, that is a lie. I knew something was wrong. I just didn't know what. I was tired all of the time, my sex drive was tanked, and I felt no enjoyment in life anymore. At the time, I was waking up at 4:30am, leaving the house at 5:30am, and driving my 17-minute journey to the office. Within those 17 minutes, I found myself numerous times falling asleep at the wheel. Not a warm fuzzy feeling when traveling at 60 mph on a dark windy highway. After my long day in the office, I would again make this trip back home only to repeat the nodding off pattern once again. This was more than just feeling depressed. After talking with my naturopathic doctor and an adrenal test, I really started to take my peace of mind and meditation practice more serious.

These physical outcomes are not separate from your emotional and psychological life—they are deeply intertwined reflections of it. And once you start listening to your body, the whole narrative begins to shift. The symptoms aren't the problem—they're the invitation.

Psychologically, this moment often aligns with what Carl Jung referred to as the "midlife transition." It's the time when the ego—your constructed identity—begins to loosen its grip, and the unconscious starts demanding to be heard. The stories that got you here no longer fit. The roles you've played start to chafe. You realize that you've been surviving, not thriving. Performing, not living.

Jennie Potter, in *Self-Sabotage No More*, echoes this inner reckoning by describing the way we develop subconscious set points early in life—beliefs and energetic limits we internalize about what we're allowed to have, feel, or become. These set points shape our autopilot behavior and keep us circling in familiar but limiting loops, even as we outgrow them.

Gay Hendricks, in *The Big Leap*, calls this our "Upper Limit Problem"—the self-imposed ceiling that kicks in when we start reaching for more joy, success, or fulfillment than our inner thermostat believes we're allowed to have. When we hit that threshold, we unconsciously sabotage, shrink, or retreat into old patterns.

So this transition isn't just existential—it's *energetic, biological, and behavioral*. In fact, for many women, this phase mirrors what some have begun calling a *second puberty*. Around age 40, a neurological and hormonal recalibration begins—a shift in brain chemistry similar to what we experienced during adolescence. Emotional processing deepens. Identity destabilizes and reforms. Old priorities dissolve. New ones surface, often unapologetically. It's not just "hormonal." It's a full-spectrum reconfiguration.

Mothers often encounter a similar shift upon entering parenthood—an accelerated transformation that affects brain chemistry, emotional bandwidth, and nervous system function. And men aren't exempt. They typically experience this awakening on a delayed timeline, often in their 50s, echoing the same developmental arc we see in adolescence—where girls mature neurologically and emotionally before boys.

This isn't you unraveling. This is your system saying: *It's time.*

You start to feel the tension between who you've been conditioned to be and who you're actually becoming. That inner friction? That's the signal. The invitation to break through—not just emotionally, but neurologically and spiritually—to your next level of truth.

This isn't about blaming the past. It's about seeing it clearly. The career you pursued, the marriage you nurtured, the identity you shaped—all of it may have served you. But it may no longer be serving who you are now. That is the core of the wake-up call: the acknowledgment that you've evolved, and your life has not kept pace.

What That Moment of Clarity Feels Like

Clarity doesn't always feel empowering at first. In fact, it often arrives with grief. You grieve the time lost, the energy spent, the parts of yourself you abandoned to be what the world asked of you. Like peeling off a skin you didn't even realize you were wearing. There is no linear path through this moment. For some, it comes in a single, striking realization. For others, it unfolds slowly over months or even years.

But regardless of the timeline, what emerges is a confrontation with truth. You begin to notice the disconnect between what you say you value and how you're actually living. You start asking deeper questions. Not just "What am I doing?" but "Who am I doing it for?" and "What do I actually want?" You might cry. You might rage. You might sit in stunned silence and wonder, "Why the hell didn't I see this sooner?"

This moment is sacred because it strips away illusion. And that's not easy. It demands honesty, courage, and the willingness to sit in discomfort. It demands that you stop gaslighting yourself, stop minimizing your needs, and start acknowledging that your dissatisfaction is not selfish—it's information. That moment of clarity doesn't solve everything. It won't hand you a perfect five-step plan. But it cracks the shell. And once that shell breaks, there's no stuffing yourself back inside it.

You start telling the truth. To yourself first. Then, to everyone else.

You start asking better questions:

WHAT DO I ACTUALLY WANT?
WHOSE LIFE HAVE I BEEN LIVING?
WHAT VERSION OF ME IS DYING TO COME ALIVE?

It's uncomfortable as hell. But it's real. And real is what you've been craving. This is the threshold. Once you cross it, you can't unknow it. You can't go back to pretending everything's fine. That door is closed. Burned down. Replaced with something unknown but true.

Why This Moment Is Pivotal

This moment—the breakdown, the breakthrough, the burn-it-all-down awakening—isn't just important. It's *everything*.

Because from here, **you stop bullshitting yourself.**

In the work I do, this moment marks the beginning of transformation. Not the superficial kind—the kind that tells you to buy a new planner, try a new diet, or change your wardrobe. This is the deep, structural kind. The kind that invites you to look at your inner architecture and ask: *What was built for survival, and what is aligned with who I actually am?*

From a neurological standpoint, your brain is wired for efficiency and comfort, not fulfillment and happiness. The longer you run patterns of behavior—people-pleasing, perfectionism, over-functioning—the more entrenched those neural pathways become. But neuroplasticity teaches us that change is always possible. The brain can be rewired. The stories can be reauthored.

Think of our old 1990s or even 80s computers. Picture that real cloth green screen and those bright colored Macs. Yes, I am fully aware I am dating myself here. Let's just get it out of the way now...I'm a product of the 80s and 90s...and LOVING EVERY BIT OF IT. Think about what would happen if we were to try to run those operating systems on our tiny laptops or smartphones today. It wouldn't work. Just like the computer companies, we have to run an update of our internal operating systems.

This is why the wake-up call matters. It's not just about wanting more—it's about realizing you were made for more. Because it's the beginning of conscious choice. It's the moment where you stop running on default and start engaging with intention. Where you move from coping to creating.

It's also the moment many people resist. Because society tells you you're crazy or in the midlife crisis, hormonal, or (and I would lay money on this) simply because it threatens the known. It asks you to let go of control, to face uncertainty, to risk being misunderstood. But here's what I've learned after decades in the mental health and coaching space: staying stuck is often more painful than stepping into the unknown. The pain of the known is quiet and cumulative. The possibility of the unknown is disruptive—but it holds freedom.

It's not a crisis. It's a compass.

Call to Integration

So here you are. Awake, uncomfortable, and uncertain. This is your threshold. Take a deep breath. Let yourself feel the friction. You don't need to have it all figured out. You just need to be willing to listen. To yourself. To the nudges, the aches, the quiet truths that have been trying to get your attention.

Ask yourself:

WHERE AM I LIVING OUT OF HABIT INSTEAD OF DESIRE?
WHAT TRUTHS HAVE I BEEN AVOIDING BECAUSE THEY WOULD REQUIRE CHANGE?
WHAT WOULD IT LOOK LIKE TO STOP SURVIVING AND START LIVING?

This is not the end of your story. It's the beginning of a new chapter. One where you don't have to perform, pretend, or prove. One where your life begins to reflect your truth.

I woke up almost to the very day I turned 40. It was like someone had flipped the switch within me. Sure, I was feeling this nagging itch years prior but I just kept up the illusion that this is normal for everyone to have health problems that were unexplained, mental health concerns unable to work through, dissatisfaction for my work. Heck, I grew up on Married...With Children, The Simpsons, Seinfeld, and many other sitcoms where the main characters (which were in their midlifes) were complaining about this, that, and everything. To me, this was normal. Life was only good in your teens and twenties. Alcohol made the rest of life tolerable.

At 40, I woke up. Like a salmon to the face. I realized my filter was gone (more than it already was eroded). I didn't quite care what people thought of me. Sure, sure. I was still concerned with how I looked but not for others...for myself to feel good about me. I started to step into my true self.

I also started to long for something more. Something real.

Now, hear me out... I. LOVE. MY. FAMILY. However...if I had known I didn't have to operate in the typical linear fashion of school, then marriage, then house, then kids, and if you are Wonder Woman add a career on top. I may have done things a bit different. Somewhere along the way I lost myself. My true self.

It's funny now thinking back on it. I have a friend that when I adopted my most amazing, wonderful, free spirited, wild child, told me "Erin, don't lose who you are. Having a kid will change you but it doesn't have to change who you are. Do the things that make you happy. That make you who you are." Those words ring in my head daily. And she was right, once I became a mom, I started to let go of some of the things that brought me joy and made me, me. However, looking back on it now, I was losing Erin long before that conversation took place.

My limited beliefs, self-sabotaging behaviors, shadows, and my personal glass ceiling were all outdated and keeping me in a place of complacency as I slowly lost who I am. The free spirited, wild child, artist, and analytic person I am deep down. To this...I want to welcome you.

Welcome to the wake-up call. You're not broken. You're breaking open.

Now let's go deeper.

Two

THE REAL REASON YOU'RE STUCK

Let's get one thing straight: **you're not stuck because you're lazy, weak, unmotivated, or broken.** You're stuck because your system is running exactly the way it was programmed to.

And spoiler alert? That programming wasn't written by the wisest, most aligned version of you. It was written by the 5-year-old you trying to survive chaos. The 12-year-old you trying to make sense of pain. The 20-something version of you trying to fit into boxes that were never made to hold you. Think about it...would you want your teenage self running the show? What were you like at 12, 13, 14, or even hell...21?

I can tell you, I was not the most responsible in those years. I was constantly worrying about whether my zit on my forehead was noticeable, daydreaming about becoming Mrs. Devon Sawa, and how I can be popular while hiding from the teasing. At 21? I was all about college, having fun, and my social life. There was nothing about functioning on a daily basis for a long prosperous life. Or about bringing balance of both work and play, productivity and inner peace, or letting my voice be heard and holding the silence.

Most of us are still operating from an outdated system—an inner script coded with shame, fear, guilt, unworthiness, people-pleasing, perfectionism, and deep, unspoken grief. And that's what we call "normal".

But it's not normal. It's just familiar.

This is the comfortability that as humans we want to live in. **We were not designed to be happy.** I know, mind blowing. We were designed to be comfortable. To live our lives in our own personal climate controlled comfort zones.

You Were Never Broken—You Were Conditioned

When you feel stuck, it's often because you're bumping up against the **set points** you unconsciously agreed to long ago. Jennie Potter calls these emotional and energetic limits—the inner thermostats that tell you how much happiness, freedom, and ease you're "allowed" to feel before sabotage kicks in. Gay Hendricks would call this your **Upper Limit Problem**—the self-imposed barrier you hit when you dare to live bigger than your old identity believes is safe.

I like to think of them as your **glass ceilings**. Individual limits you have set within your life. You can see through them and see what it could look like for you above that ceiling, but you are unable to just simply walk through it. You don't just have one glass ceiling. You have many. Depending on the situation or goal; you could have a glass ceiling around finances, physical health, relationships, career opportunities, etc. and within each of these, you may have another subset of glass ceilings. They are emotional and energetic, not a physical wall but one that you tend to stay stuck behind while the rest of the world is still moving.

And when you try to break past that ceiling? The alarms go off. Cue the shutdown, the panic, the procrastination, the over-thinking, the sudden urge to burn it all down. Sometimes, this is a very noticeable, visceral reaction such as a panic attack. But more common, it is a silent alarm that triggers you to find some way to stop the production line. Ever find yourself doom-scrolling for hours after coming up with a really great idea for a side hustle that sends tingles up through your spine? Or do you continue to do all of the work to lose that last ten pounds only to find it sticking to you like a colicky infant?

To aid in this round-about, take a look at Figure 2.1. You are strolling along when all of the sudden the light bulb turns on. Maybe it is an amazing idea or a deep desire for change. You get excited for this new possibility. Energetically, however, you start to smash up against the glass ceiling and when you start to think about breaking through that glass barrier, the silent alarm rings loud to your subconscious. This releases a number of emotions, thoughts, and feelings. Some are happy and wonderful. Others are not so joyous. The limited beliefs start to chatter, you find yourself sabotaging the efforts, and the shadow self is in control, halting everything you were thinking of doing. But there is good news, it does bring you back to your "comfort zone". Okay...maybe it really isn't a good thing as then nothing changes. Eventually, you forget that you tried this and life continues. The process is then repeated with you having that spark once again.

That's not failure. That's your nervous system doing exactly what it was trained to do: **keep you small, because small felt safe and safe is comfortable.**

Figure 2.1 My scribbles about the process of how you keep getting stuck and staying in your comfort zone.

But just because it feels safe doesn't mean it's right or that it is in your best or highest interest. It just means it's familiar. And the nervous system prioritizes familiarity over fulfillment every damn time—until you rewire it.

The Autopilot is Running the Show

The brain is efficient as hell. Once it learns how to survive a situation, it files the pattern and puts it on repeat. What starts as protection becomes a habit. What begins as a coping mechanism becomes your default identity.

You think you're choosing your job, your relationships, your daily habits—but if you've never questioned the programming underneath, you're probably not choosing at all.

You're reacting. You're surviving. You're on autopilot.

Autopilot isn't just forgetting why you walked into a room or zoning out during your morning commute. It's a *whole identity system*—a subconscious program built from survival strategies, belief systems, family patterns, and cultural conditioning that runs the show when you're not consciously paying attention.

Jennie Potter describes this as running your life manually—but based on programming written in crisis, confusion, or emotional suppression. You may be driving the car, but the GPS is glitching. You're swerving toward old destinations you don't even want anymore.

You ghost opportunities. You pick fights. You forget to reply to the email that could've changed your career. You go numb with Netflix and Oreos. You shrink—not because you're weak, but because your system doesn't know what safety looks like at a higher frequency.

Gay Hendricks frames this as the "Upper Limit Problem"—that place where your nervous system starts freaking out the moment you step into expansion. Because while your *soul* might crave growth, your body is trying to protect the known.

Abraham Hicks would say you're holding a vibrational habit. A practiced energy pattern that reinforces what you already believe about yourself. So even when your desires change, your frequency doesn't. That's why you can want something deeply... and still keep manifesting the same old shit.

Where the Autopilot Began

Autopilot isn't random. It was programmed.

Not by one moment, but by thousands—usually when you were young, impressionable, and just trying to make sense of a world that didn't always feel safe, fair, or nurturing. Now, I will say that a single traumatic event can also mold our operating system. Events such as child abuse, sexual assault, experiencing a devastating natural disaster, or witnessing a violent crime could leave a very powerful impact on how you later engage in the world around you and what you may say about your own thoughts or actions.

As a child, your brain was like a sponge—and your nervous system? Wide open. You weren't just absorbing your environment. You were *wiring yourself around it.* Through your observations and interactions with your parents, friends, other adults, and society you were collecting little nuggets of how the world *around you* worked.

You learned:

How love was earned (or withheld).
What emotions were "acceptable" and which ones made people uncomfortable.
What version of you got praised.
When to speak up... and when to stay small.

Maybe you learned to be the fixer, the achiever, the peacemaker, or the invisible one. Maybe you learned that emotions made things worse, or that asking for what you need was a guaranteed letdown.

Those early experiences built your operating system. Not consciously. Not maliciously. Just *automatically* as a means to keep you feeling safe and comfortable.

Neuroscience tells us that by the time we're around 12 years old, most of our subconscious operating system is already in place.

The emotional reflexes, belief patterns, and default responses you operate from today were wired through early relational experiences—before you had the maturity or power to fully understand them. Unless we become conscious of those old codes, we end up living out the same emotional loops and behavioral scripts on autopilot... even decades later.

For me personally, I have noticed that much of my own programming was hardwired between ages 9-12 with a dash of 5 years of age. This was a time of my parents getting a divorce, taking on a new role as "surrogate parent" with my younger brother, my father later getting remarried, blending another family into what I was starting to call my "normal", and then all of the traumas that came with psychological abuse (although probably unintentional, still fucked me up). I also witnessed my mother go through a very painful accident involving being burnt all over her body when I was about 10 years old. Each of these events, the small particles of stress dusted on life during this time, carved out the paths I would take later in my life.

I want to go a bit deeper here...That happened when I was let's say conservatively by 12 years of age. At the time of writing this book, I am 43 years old. I have then been walking this world with programming that is 31 years old. Would you use a computer that was 31 years old and have it function in the work that we have today? Hell no. I'm talking like working with the old Apple II computers with the floppy disks and real cloth green screen. Although it was great at the time and did wonders in the 80s. It is missing out on all that has changed. All that has been learnt along the way.

So when we talk about "autopilot," we're not blaming you or your parents or society even. We're naming the invisible system that's been driving the bus.

Autopilot is sneaky. It wears the mask of responsibility. Of being "realistic." Of keeping the peace. But underneath it? Is programming. And here's the kicker: most of it was wired in long before you had the power to choose otherwise.

But now you do.

That's where this work begins—not with shame, but with awareness. Not with tearing yourself down, but with finally seeing the architecture of who you've been... so you can consciously become who you actually are. And that's where the Mindshift begins—not in massive change, but in the moment you *interrupt* the unconscious cycle.

Your Brain Is Filtering Everything (RAS)

Here's a wild truth: your brain filters out almost all the information coming at you—millions of bits per second. You're not consciously aware of most of it, and that's a good thing. Otherwise, you'd be overwhelmed. What do you notice? That's curated by something called the **Reticular Activating System (RAS)**.

Think of the RAS as your brain's bouncer, deciding what gets past the velvet rope into your awareness. And how does it decide? Based on what your subconscious believes is important, relevant, or emotionally charged. In other words, the RAS is deeply influenced by your internal programming. What you think, feel, expect, and believe determines what you actually see.

Let's say you're thinking about buying a red Jeep. Suddenly, you see red Jeeps everywhere. Were they always there? Yep. Did you only just now start noticing them? Exactly. That's the RAS at work. It filters in the information that matches what your brain has tagged as "relevant."

Now imagine what happens when your emotional state is consistently negative. If you feel stuck, unworthy, overwhelmed, or fearful, your RAS will helpfully filter in evidence that confirms those emotions. If your subconscious is carrying beliefs like, "I always mess things up" or "Nothing ever works for me," your brain will pick up on situations, words, facial expressions—anything that confirms those thoughts—and conveniently ignore or downplay anything that contradicts them.

This is how the loop continues. Thoughts rooted in emotion influence what your brain notices, which reinforces the emotional state, which then feeds more of the same kinds of thoughts. Rinse and repeat.

But here's the good news: you can change what your RAS filters in. You can train your brain to look for evidence of possibility, support, and growth. It starts with regulating your emotional state. When you calm your nervous system, practice presence, and engage in energetic or somatic work, you send signals to your brain that say, "Hey, we're safe now. You can let in something new."

This is why practices like energy healing, breathwork, meditation, and body-based awareness matter. They're not just trendy wellness tools. They recondition your internal environment so your RAS can recalibrate. And when your filter changes, your reality starts to shift too.

So the next time you catch yourself saying, "See? It always goes wrong for me," pause. Ask yourself: is that true, or is it just what your brain has been trained to notice?

What you look for, you will find. And when you start looking for proof of your power, your healing, your resilience, and your worth—that's what you'll start seeing more of. The world doesn't change. But the way you experience it does.

Energy, Belief, and Behavior—They're All Connected

As Dr. Joe Dispenza writes in *Becoming Supernatural*, we are not just emotional beings—we are electromagnetic fields walking around reacting to the past. Our thoughts send signals out; our emotions draw experiences back in. The body becomes addicted to familiar emotional states like stress, worry, and guilt, and unless we change our internal environment, our external reality stays on rinse and repeat. This is why elevated emotional states—like gratitude, love, and joy—aren't just feel-good fluff. They're the building blocks for shifting our biology and tuning into a different frequency of possibility.

John Ruskan echoes this in *Emotional Clearing*, reminding us that unresolved emotional energy isn't just stored in our memory—it's stored in the body. He emphasizes that to truly release sabotage patterns, we can't just think differently. We have to feel differently. Deeply. Fully. Without judgment. It's not about analyzing your way to clarity—it's about allowing what's there to move through.

So if you've been "doing the work" and still feel stuck? You're not broken. You're just not working at the level where the real shifts happen yet. Because the surface has shifted, but the wiring underneath hasn't.

Here's where we connect the dots: you can't mindset your way out of sabotage if the **energy underneath** is still in survival mode. You can't affirm your way to wholeness if you don't believe you're worthy of it. You can't organize your way out of burnout if your nervous system doesn't feel safe resting.

This is why so many people "do the work" and still feel stuck. Because the surface has shifted, but the **wiring underneath hasn't**. There are still energetic blockages, fears, limiting beliefs that are clogging your path to what you are truly wanting for your life. Until you interrupt the pattern—emotionally, somatically, and energetically—you'll keep recreating the same loops. Different faces. Different settings. Same damn story.

Breaking The Loop

If you've been wondering why your affirmations aren't working... Why you keep circling back to the same job, the same toxic relationship, the same patterns of burnout or procrastination... It's not because you're broken. It's because you've been running a program that was installed before you were old enough to question it. And the more you try to force your way out of it without naming the source, the harder the pattern grips.

You start to realize that what you've been calling "just the way I am" is actually just... old wiring. Old reactions. Outdated reflexes. The parts of you that learned how to keep the peace, stay invisible, stay safe.

That's the autopilot.

And here's where the mind-fuck deepens: once we start pulling back the curtain on this wiring, we see something even sneakier lurking beneath it all... Sabotage.

Self-sabotage isn't just bad behavior. **It's brilliant survival.** It's not laziness. It's not weakness. It's not some character flaw you need to fix. It's your nervous system saying, *"This is as far as I know how to go without dying."*

That job you stayed in too long? That relationship you didn't walk away from? That dream you never chased? It wasn't because you didn't want more. It's because somewhere along the way, you were taught—*maybe not with words, but with consequences*—that having more came with danger. That being seen would get you hurt. That success meant isolation. That rest meant punishment. That being your full damn self would cost you love, safety, or belonging.

So you learned to hit the brakes. To self-destruct just enough to stay in the comfort zone. To get "almost there," then pull back right before it got good.

And let's be clear: that part of you isn't evil. It's not the villain in your story. It's the part that kept you alive. That made sure you fit in. That helped you survive the chaos, the judgment, the abandonment. But you're not that kid anymore. You're not in that house, or that relationship, or that old system. You have *power* now. Awareness. Choice.

And now that you're waking up, that old survival pattern is starting to feel like a cage. One you've outgrown. We'll go deeper into sabotage in the next chapter—because once you start to name the ways you unconsciously hold yourself back, everything starts to shift.

But for now, just let this truth settle in:

You're not broken. You're just running an outdated survival program. And once you see it for what it is, you finally get to choose:

Do I keep the pattern, or do I rewrite the code?

Three

Naming the Saboteur

L et's just call it out: self-sabotage is one sneaky bastard. It doesn't always wear a mask or scream into the void. Most of the time, it whispers sweet nothings disguised as logic. It sounds like: "Now's not the right time." "I just need to get more organized first." "Maybe I'm not cut out for this." You convince yourself you're being reasonable—when really, you're being hijacked by an outdated internal program that's trying to keep you safe... by keeping you small...like the child you once were.

Let's go back to where we left off in Chapter Two. We talked about the inner operating system—your autopilot—and how it was built long before you had the tools, awareness, or agency to know what the hell you were doing. That operating system didn't just help you survive. It became the blueprint for how you interpret life. And tucked inside that blueprint? Is the saboteur.

This isn't about shaming yourself. Quite the opposite, actually. It's about finally meeting that inner saboteur with honesty and compassion. Because here's the hard truth wrapped in grace: your sabotage was never about failing. It was about protecting yourself.

Let's talk about the saboteur—the sneaky, well-dressed, sweet-talking voice in your head that's been whispering lies since you were old enough to make meaning out of chaos. You know the one. It's the reason you start questioning your decisions right after you make them. It's the reason you don't send the email, don't launch the project, don't walk away from the job or relationship you know is draining you. And here's the twist: it's not trying to ruin your life. It thinks it's saving it.

The saboteur is smart. It learned early that keeping you small meant keeping you safe. It's the internalized voice of past pain, wrapped in the disguise of protection. But don't be fooled by the velvet gloves. It's running the whole damn show if you don't name it. And to name it, we have to go deeper. Way deeper.

We're not talking about a single personality flaw or a bad habit. We're talking about the culmination of years—decades—of survival wiring. Think of the saboteur as your internal defense attorney, filing every piece of evidence it can to convince you why you shouldn't do the thing that threatens your current identity.

This chapter is your invitation to start listening differently. To start identifying the saboteur not as a villain to be punished, but as a wounded part of you that's been calling the shots without your consent.

You're not broken. You're just becoming conscious.

Self-Sabotage Isn't Stupidity—It's Strategy

You don't procrastinate because you're lazy. You do it because finishing the task would mean stepping into visibility—and with that, the risk of being judged, misunderstood, or rejected. You don't pick the same dead-end relationships or toxic work dynamics because you're a slow learner. You do it because, on some deep, unconscious level, the chaos feels familiar... and familiar feels safe.

Self-sabotage isn't a lack of willpower. It's not a moral failing. It's not because you're "just not wired for success." It's strategy—survival-level brilliance coded into your nervous system when you were too young to know better.

Let's be real: if you learned early that love was conditional, that being too loud got you punished, or that expressing your needs led to disappointment, your system took notes. It started building rules, scripts, and guardrails to keep you "safe." And while those rules might have helped you stay afloat in the past, they're now anchoring you to a version of yourself you've outgrown.

This is your system doing its job. That job just happens to be outdated.

Sabotage shows up as that moment you ghost the opportunity you've been praying for. The second-guessing after you finally speak your truth. The tension in your chest when someone praises you, and instead of feeling seen, you feel exposed. It's not because you're weak—it's because there's a part of you that believes thriving will cost you something you're not ready to lose: love, safety, belonging.

So let's make this clear—self-sabotage is not stupidity. It's the armor you built to survive a world that once told you your fullness was too much. But you're not in that world anymore. And the armor? It's starting to chafe.

Self-sabotage is brilliant. Not joyful, not healthy, not liberating. But brilliant.

It's your system—emotional, mental, and energetic—doing *exactly* what it was trained to do: survive.

Even if that survival comes at the cost of your fulfillment, expansion, or happiness.

How It Shows Up (Even When You Swear You're "Fine")

Sabotage doesn't always come in like a wrecking ball. Sometimes, it tiptoes in dressed like a to-do list. Sometimes it looks like perfectionism or overcommitment. Other times it wears the face of burnout, apathy, or that voice that whispers, "Maybe next week."

"Look over there...at that mom that is doing it all. Career, after-school activities, weekend events with the family, cleans the house, and provides the meals on the table. She is such a multi-tasker. Yep, a real go-getter." What we may not see is the layers of lotions and serums she has under that thick concealer hiding her tiredness, loneliness, fear, and sadness.

It's easy to think of sabotage as something dramatic or destructive, but let's get real—it's usually subtle. It's camouflaged in your routines, your "responsible choices," and the chaos you've convinced yourself is just part of being an adult.

Here's what sabotage actually looks like in the wild:

- **Procrastination:** You tell yourself you "work better under pressure," but it's fear of failure (or success) that's got its foot on the brake.

- **Perfectionism:** You endlessly tweak, polish, plan—because launching something flawed feels more dangerous than not launching at all. Again, another fear such as failure or success but let's also add in rejection to this one.

- **Over-functioning:** You're the one who holds it all together for everyone else, which conveniently keeps you too busy to face your own shit.

- **People-pleasing:** You say yes when your body screams no. You smile through resentment because you're terrified of being perceived as difficult.

- **Numbing out:** You scroll, snack, shop, or stay "busy" to avoid sitting with what's really bubbling under the surface.

And we normalize all of it.

We say things like, "That's just how I am," or "It's just a busy season," or "It's not the right time." But what's actually happening under the surface is sabotage—stealth mode.

Then come the archetypes—because self-sabotage isn't just behavior, it's an identity you slip into like a favorite old hoodie. Cozy. Familiar. Limiting as hell.

Let's name the saboteur's favorite disguises:

NOTE FROM YOUR AUTHOR—

Before you start down this next part, I highly recommend you take a breather, grab a snacky snack, or even take a bathroom break. You are about to dive into a section of this book that can take time to go through. If you are brave, go right in. However, there is no shame in scanning through the next several pages and then go back to read up on the ones that tickled your fancy. You won't get any judgement from me. With that said...bon appétit. You have been warned. Game on.

THE PERFECTIONIST

- *What it looks like:* You obsess over details, rewrite emails ten times, or delay launching your project because it's "not quite ready." You create impossible standards for yourself (and sometimes others) and then spiral when you can't meet them. You measure your worth by how flawless your performance appears—never by how honest or human you are.

- *What's underneath:* Fear of failure. Fear of rejection. Fear of being seen as "less than." A belief that you have to earn love, success, or safety by being exceptional at all times. Perfection becomes your armor—because vulnerability feels too risky.

- *Core wound:* "If I'm not perfect, I'm unworthy." Or: "If I fail, I'll be rejected."

- *Emotional roots:* Anxiety. Shame. Conditional self-worth. Chronic pressure. Deep sadness that you've never felt safe just being you.

- *The truth:* Perfection is an illusion. What people connect with isn't flawlessness—it's authenticity. The cracks are where the light gets in. Perfectionism doesn't protect you; it imprisons you. You don't need to earn your worth through constant polishing—you were worthy the moment you showed up in this world. Progress, not perfection, is where transformation lives.

THE MARTYR

- *What it looks like:* You're always the one who says yes. You pick up the slack, carry the emotional load, and wear your self-sacrifice like a badge of honor. You give until there's nothing left—and then you give some more. Resentment simmers beneath the surface, but you push it down. You're exhausted, but admitting that feels selfish.

- *What's underneath:* Fear of abandonment. A belief that your needs don't matter. You've internalized the idea that love must be earned through selflessness, and that setting boundaries means you're failing as a friend, partner, or parent.

- *Core wound:* "If I have needs, I'll be seen as selfish." Or: "If I take up space, I'll lose my place."

- *Emotional roots:* Guilt. Resentment. Suppressed anger. Loneliness. A deep craving to be nurtured—but no roadmap for receiving.

- *The truth:* Your worth is not measured by how much you suffer for others. Taking care of yourself is not selfish—it's essential. Love built on self-erasure is not love; it's survival. You're allowed to receive. You're allowed to rest. You're allowed to matter. When you honor your needs, you teach others to do the same—and that's the kind of ripple effect the world needs more of.

THE CHAMELEON

- *What it looks like:* You blend in. You read the room, then become whatever version of yourself will be most accepted. You downplay your truth, shift your tone, and hide your edges so you don't make waves. You're the peacekeeper, the shape-shifter, the one who never causes trouble. You pride yourself on being "easygoing," but inside, you feel invisible.

- *What's underneath:* Fear of rejection. A core belief that your authentic self is too much—or not enough. You've learned that belonging comes through adaptation, not authenticity.

- *Core wound:* "If I'm my true self, I won't be loved."

- *Emotional roots:* Insecurity. Loneliness. Identity confusion. Emotional abandonment. A chronic sense of being disconnected from who you really are.

- *The truth:* You don't have to perform to be worthy. The real you—the bold, messy, honest, opinionated, weird, wonderful you—is the only version worth building a life around. The right people don't need you to dilute your truth to keep them comfortable. When you stop shape-shifting, you start belonging—not just to others, but to yourself. And that's where freedom lives.

THE REBEL

- *What it looks like:* You resist rules, push back on expectations, and refuse to be told what to do—even when the "rules" are your own goals. You pride yourself on being independent and unconventional, but sometimes you sabotage progress just to avoid feeling controlled. You start things with fire, then burn them down when they start to feel confining.

- *What's underneath:* Fear of losing autonomy. Deep resistance to authority. A belief that compliance equals weakness or erasure. Often, rebellion is a trauma response rooted in feeling powerless.

- *Core wound:* "If I follow the rules, I'll lose myself."

- *Emotional roots:* Defiance. Anger. Hyper-independence. Grief over past times when your voice, power, or choices were suppressed.

- *The truth:* Freedom isn't the absence of responsibility—it's the ability to choose your path with intention. You don't have to burn it all down to stay true to yourself. Structure isn't your enemy; it can actually be the container that allows your wildness to thrive. You can be powerful and grounded. You can lead with your fire without scorching your own progress.

THE CRITIC

- *What it looks like:* You constantly pick yourself apart—your body, your work, your decisions, your worth. You hold impossibly high standards and speak to yourself in ways you'd never speak to someone else. Even small wins are minimized or dismissed. There's always something that could've been better, faster, smarter, more impressive.

- *What's underneath:* Fear of vulnerability. Fear of being exposed or judged. A belief that relentless self-policing will shield you from external attack or disappointment. Often formed in environments where praise was conditional—or where criticism came faster than love.

- *Core wound:* "If I hurt me first, others won't get the chance."

- *Emotional roots:* Shame. Deep sadness. Hypervigilance. Perfectionism. Chronic self-doubt masked as "realism."

- *The truth:* Self-attack doesn't make you stronger—it

makes you smaller. You weren't born thinking you weren't enough. That was taught, modeled, and internalized. But now? You get to unlearn it. Compassion isn't weakness—it's power. The more you speak to yourself with kindness, the less room your critic has to grow. You don't have to be perfect to be worthy. You don't have to be flawless to be lovable. You're allowed to be human—and still be extraordinary.

THE ESCAPE ARTIST

- *What it looks like:* You bail—physically, emotionally, or mentally—when life starts to feel overwhelming. You ghost projects, dodge hard conversations, retreat from responsibilities, and numb out with food, Netflix, alcohol, or spiritual bypassing. You chase newness, distraction, or anything that lets you avoid the discomfort of staying present.

- *What's underneath:* Fear of failure. Fear of being exposed as not enough. Deep emotional exhaustion. A belief that if you stay in the discomfort too long, you'll drown in it. Escaping becomes your way of self-protection—because confronting the mess feels too risky.

- *Core wound:* "If I stay, I'll get hurt." Or: "If I face this, I won't survive it."

- *Emotional roots:* Overwhelm. Panic. Avoidance. Learned helplessness. Loneliness. You may have learned early that big emotions weren't safe or that your needs weren't met when you expressed them—so now, you just disappear. Even from yourself.

- *The truth:* Running only delays the reckoning. But here's the thing—there's no shame in needing a break. You learned to escape because staying present once felt too hard, too unsafe. But now, you're stronger than you think. Presence doesn't have to mean pressure. It can mean power. When you stop abandoning yourself and start showing up—even in baby steps—you prove to your nervous system that you can handle it. You can feel the discomfort and still move forward. You don't have to run to be safe. You can root instead.

THE OVERACHIEVER

- *What it looks like:* You're always in motion—juggling a packed calendar, chasing goals, checking boxes, collecting gold stars. Rest feels like failure. Slowing down triggers guilt. Even when you hit a milestone, you're already onto the next one. You measure your worth by your productivity. If you're not achieving something, you don't know who you are. You may look "successful" on the outside, but inside? You're exhausted, anxious, and secretly afraid that if you ever stopped, the whole illusion would crumble.

- *What's underneath:* A deep-seated fear of being ordinary, invisible, or unworthy without proof of your value.

Somewhere along the line, you learned that being loved or respected required achievement. You equated accomplishment with approval and being busy with being safe. You crave validation, but can't seem to feel it when it comes.

- *Core wound:* "If I'm not doing something extraordinary, I don't matter."

- *Emotional roots:* Burnout from chronic overdrive. Anxiety that rest equals regression. An inner emptiness masked by constant motion. Guilt that arises the moment you try to prioritize your well-being.

- *The truth:* You are worthy even when you're not producing. You are valuable even when you're not achieving. The love you're chasing with your to-do list can't be earned—it's something you already deserve. Your worth isn't a performance metric. You don't have to prove yourself through exhaustion. When you learn to rest without guilt, to say no without justification, and to celebrate without conditions, you reclaim a kind of power that no trophy can give you. You're not a machine. You're a miracle. And you deserve to feel that.

THE JOKESTER

- *What it looks like:* You're the life of the party, the one with the sharp wit and the perfect comeback. You keep things light, funny, and entertaining—but never too

41

deep. If the conversation starts inching toward real feelings, you crack a joke. When someone compliments you, you brush it off with sarcasm. You make yourself the punchline before anyone else can. Vulnerability makes your skin crawl, so you wear humor like armor.

- *What's underneath:* A deep fear of being seen—truly seen—and rejected. Somewhere along the way, you learned that emotions were dangerous, that softness made you a target. Humor became your shield. It helped you belong without getting hurt. You could show up without ever actually showing yourself.

- *Core wound:* "If I let people see the real me—my pain, my fear, my heart—they'll think I'm weak, or worse... they'll walk away."

- *Emotional roots:* Fear of vulnerability. Repressed sadness. A deep ache for connection buried beneath layers of irony. Loneliness masked as charm. Shame wrapped in a one-liner.

- *The truth:* Your humor is a gift, but it's not your only one. You don't have to entertain to be worthy of love. You don't have to laugh through your pain to be strong. The most magnetic thing about you isn't your ability to make others laugh—it's your willingness to let them see you. When you let people in beyond the punchline, you invite true intimacy. And that connection? It's what you've really been craving all along. You're allowed to be the joke and the truth. You're allowed to feel it all—and still be enough.

THE CYNIC

- *What it looks like:* You side-eye optimism, roll your eyes at vision boards, and have a snarky comeback for every motivational quote. You don't dare get your hopes up—because in your experience, hope only leads to disappointment. You might laugh off your jadedness as "just being realistic," but deep down, you've built a fortress around your heart. Optimism feels like a setup. So you kill the dream before it has a chance to break your heart.

- *What's underneath:* Old heartbreak. Deep disappointment. Times you dared to believe, to try, to open… and got slammed shut in return. Your cynicism is armor. It's protection wrapped in sarcasm. You've convinced yourself it's safer not to hope at all than to risk the gut punch of letdown.

- *Core wound:* "Every time I've hoped, I've been hurt. So I won't make that mistake again."

- *Emotional roots:* Grief. Resentment. Disillusionment. Protective pessimism. Emotional fatigue from past failures or betrayals.

- *The truth:* Your protectiveness is understandable. You've been burned. You've seen things fall apart. But your cynicism isn't saving you—it's starving you. Starving your dreams, your connections, your capacity for joy. You weren't born skeptical. You became that way to survive heartbreak. But you don't have to live there anymore. Let yourself hope again—not blindly, but bravely. Because allowing light in doesn't make you foolish. It makes you free.

THE HEALER

- *What it looks like:* You're the go-to support person, always holding space, offering guidance, or giving advice. You might be a coach, therapist, energy worker—or just the emotionally responsible one in your family or friend group. You show up for everyone... but quietly avoid your own healing. You pour endlessly into others, but your own well is bone dry.

- *What's underneath:* A deep fear of confronting your own wounds. Helping others provides purpose and validation—it makes you feel valuable and in control. If you stop and look inward, you fear what might unravel. There's safety in staying in service mode because it distracts from your own emotional backlog.

- *Core wound:* "If I stop fixing others, I'll have to face what I've buried. And I'm not sure I can handle it."

- *Emotional roots:* Codependency. Suppressed grief. Emotional exhaustion. Unacknowledged anger. A learned belief that love must be earned through usefulness.

- *The truth:* You don't have to earn your place through service. Being needed isn't the same as being loved. And no matter how powerful your healing gifts are for others, they don't exempt you from your own journey. Your wounds deserve just as much care as anyone else's. The healer heals best when they stop hiding behind the work and start doing their own.

THE VICTIM

- *What it looks like:* You feel powerless, chronically mis-understood, and convinced that life happens to you. You replay injustices, gather evidence of why things never work out, and wait for rescue—or vindication.

- *What's underneath:* Deep-seated feelings of helplessness. A belief that power equals danger or that agency will lead to blame. Staying stuck feels safer than risking empow-erment.

- *Core wound:* "If I take responsibility, it means I deserved what happened."

- *Emotional roots:* Grief. Powerlessness. Unprocessed trauma. Buried anger disguised as hopelessness.

- *The truth:* You've endured real pain. That part is valid. But healing begins when you recognize that your story doesn't have to define your future. You're not powerless—you've just been carrying your power in hidden places. The world doesn't owe you redemption; but you owe yourself liberation. You're allowed to shift from surviving to creating. Victimhood isn't your identity. It was a chapter. Now it's time to write a new one.

THE PEOPLE-PLEASER

- *What it looks like:* You say yes when you mean no. You avoid conflict like the plague. You're constantly scanning the room to make sure everyone's okay—especially with you. Your own needs, opinions, and desires get buried under the pressure to be agreeable, easygoing, and "nice." You often feel resentful, drained, or invisible, but push those feelings aside to keep the peace.

- *What's underneath:* Fear of rejection. Fear of abandonment. A belief that love must be earned through self-sacrifice and compliance. Often formed in environments where love was conditional or where conflict led to emotional withdrawal or punishment.

- *Core wound:* "If I disappoint them, I'll lose them."

- *Emotional roots:* Anxiety. Insecurity. Repressed anger. Loneliness. Chronic guilt.

- *The truth:* Your sensitivity is a gift—but not when it's weaponized against you. Pleasing others at the cost of your truth is not kindness—it's self-abandonment.

You're not too much. You're not selfish for having boundaries. In fact, your power lies in your ability to speak your needs with love and clarity. You weren't born to be liked by everyone—you were born to be you. Fully. Unapologetically. And the right people? They'll love you because of that.

THE SHADOW QUEEN/KING

- *What it looks like:* You operate from behind the scenes—pulling strings, manipulating outcomes, and keeping emotional walls sky-high. You crave power, control, or superiority to mask the deep fear of vulnerability. You may be magnetic, mysterious, even wise—but you rarely let people get too close. You use sarcasm, emotional detachment, or intellectual dominance to stay in charge and untouched.

- *What's underneath:* Fear of betrayal. Fear of being seen and rejected for who you truly are. A belief that if you let your guard down, you'll be humiliated, abandoned, or annihilated emotionally. Often formed in environments where vulnerability was punished or seen as weakness.

- *Core wound:* "If they see the real me, they'll destroy me."

- *Emotional roots:* Distrust. Hypervigilance. Emotional isolation. Suppressed grief. Pride as armor.

- *The truth:* Your depth and discernment are sacred

47

gifts—but true power isn't found in control; it's found in intimacy. You don't have to play chess with every interaction to stay safe. You don't have to carry the weight of watching every angle. You are safe to soften. You are safe to be seen. True royalty doesn't rule from fear—it leads with rooted clarity, wisdom, and heart. You don't need a throne built from walls. You need a circle that sees your whole self—and stays.

THE GOOD GIRL / GOLDEN CHILD

- *What it looks like:* You follow the rules, stay pleasant, don't ruffle feathers, and strive to be everything to everyone. You likely got praised for being "easy," "sweet," "helpful," or "mature for your age." Now, you keep the peace at all costs—even if it means silencing your truth or abandoning your own desires. You may be successful on the outside, but internally, you're exhausted and unsure who you really are.

- *What's underneath:* Fear of disappointing others. Fear of being unloved if you show anything messy, angry, or real. A belief that love is conditional—earned only through performance, obedience, and perfection.

- *Core wound:* "If I'm not good, I'll be rejected."

- *Emotional roots:* Guilt. Suppressed anger. Identity confusion. Chronic anxiety about "getting it right."

- *The truth:* You don't have to keep proving your worth. You are more than the grades, the titles, the accolades, or the approval of others. You are allowed to be human—messy, raw, real, and still loved. Your true value isn't found in how well you perform; it's found in how fully you show up as yourself. You get to rest. You get to say no. You get to disappoint people and still be good. The pedestal was never your home—it was your prison.

THE LONE WOLF

- *What it looks like:* You pride yourself on doing everything on your own. You downplay your needs, view vulnerability as weakness and rarely ask for help. You're independent to a fault—often isolating yourself emotionally, even in relationships. You might tell yourself you don't need anyone, but deep down, there's a craving to be deeply seen and supported.

- *What's underneath:* Fear of being let down. Fear of dependence. A belief that needing others is dangerous or shameful.

- *Core wound:* "If I rely on anyone, I'll be disappointed or abandoned."

- *Emotional roots:* Isolation. Distrust. Suppressed longing for connection.

- *The truth:* You were never meant to go it alone. True

strength isn't about isolation—it's about discernment. You can choose connection without losing yourself. You can lean without collapsing. You can be supported without being controlled. You don't have to earn love by proving how little you need it. Let yourself be seen. Let yourself be held. Healing happens in relationships—not in exile.

THE CONTROL FREAK

- *What it looks like:* You micromanage everything—your schedule, your space, your relationships. You have a plan for the plan and struggle when things feel uncertain or out of order. Control brings you a sense of safety, even if it's exhausting. You might disguise it as being "organized" or "responsible," but underneath it's driven by fear.

- *What's underneath:* Fear of chaos. Fear of failure. A deep discomfort with unpredictability or vulnerability.

- *Core wound:* "If I'm not in control, everything will fall apart."

- *Emotional roots:* Anxiety. Hypervigilance. Deep-seated fear of powerlessness.

- *The truth:* Control is an illusion. You never had it—not really. What you crave isn't control; it's certainty, stability, and trust. But real safety doesn't come from managing the external. It comes from trusting your internal strength. From knowing that no matter what life throws at you, you can handle it. Letting go isn't weakness—it's wisdom. Surrender isn't giving up—it's giving in to your power.

THE ISOLATOR

- *What it looks like:* You retreat when things get hard—or even when they're going well. You ghost texts, cancel plans, and pull into your own little cocoon where nothing can touch you. You might tell yourself you're just "recharging," but deep down, you know it's more than that. It's about hiding.

- *What's underneath:* Fear of vulnerability. Fear of being seen too deeply. A belief that closeness equals pain, and that emotional self-sufficiency is the only safe path.

- *Core wound:* "If I let people in, I'll be hurt, rejected, or abandoned."

- *Emotional roots:* Loneliness. Grief. A history of emotional neglect, betrayal, or trauma. Learned self-protection from a world that felt unsafe or overwhelming.

- *The truth:* Solitude can be sacred. But isolation is different—it's a survival strategy dressed in the language of independence. You weren't meant to go it alone. You're wired for connection. The very thing you fear—being seen—is also the thing that will heal you. Letting others witness you in your truth isn't weakness. It's your comeback.

THE CONTROLLER

- *What it looks like:* You micromanage every detail, have a plan (and a backup plan for the backup plan), and struggle to delegate. If something feels uncertain, you grip tighter—whether it's in relationships, projects, or your own healing journey.

- *What's underneath:* Fear of chaos. A deeply ingrained belief that if you're not in control, everything will fall apart—and it will be your fault. The Controller often stems from early experiences of instability, unpredictability, or betrayal, where control became a survival tool.

- *Core wound:* "If I let go, everything will fall apart—and I'll get hurt."

- *Emotional roots:* Hypervigilance. Anxiety. Distrust. A low-level hum of panic that feels normal. There's often a deep inner loneliness here, too, masked by the illusion of strength.

- *The truth:* The Controller isn't trying to be difficult—they're trying to prevent pain. It believes that staying in charge is the only way to stay safe. But control is a false god. It creates a temporary illusion of safety while slowly suffocating your capacity for trust, spontaneity, and ease. True power doesn't come from gripping harder. It comes from learning to feel safe even when you're not steering the wheel.

THE ROMANTICIZER

- *What it looks like:* You idealize people, relationships, or future scenarios. You get swept up in fantasies—whether it's the "perfect" partner, job, or life—and then crash hard when reality doesn't match the dream. You're always chasing the next "this time it'll be different" moment.

- *What's underneath:* Avoidance of present pain. A longing for rescue, completion, or escape. The Romanticizer often forms from early experiences of emotional neglect or inconsistency, where fantasy became a refuge and hope was the only safe drug.

- *Core wound:* "If I can just find the right person/opportunity, I'll finally be okay."

- *Emotional roots:* Longing. Disappointment. Abandonment wounds. Escapism masked as optimism. There's a deep craving for connection—but also a fear of the messiness that real intimacy requires.

- *The truth:* The Romanticizer isn't naive—they're

heart-hungry. They learned to find safety in the imagined future instead of the unpredictable now. But healing doesn't happen in daydreams—it happens in the grounded, gritty truth of the present moment. Wholeness isn't something (or someone) you find out there. It's something you build in here.

THE ANALYZER

- *What it looks like:* You overthink everything. You research every option, play out every possible outcome, and struggle to make decisions because you're trapped in a loop of "what ifs." You seek certainty before action—but the more you analyze, the more paralyzed you become.

- *What's underneath:* Fear of making the wrong move. Fear of regret. A deep need for control, rooted in environments where unpredictability or punishment made mistakes feel dangerous or humiliating.

- *Core wound:* "If I choose wrong, everything will fall apart—and it will be my fault."

- *Emotional roots:* Anxiety. Doubt. Control. Perfectionism in disguise. There's often a buried grief over missed opportunities and the shame of perceived "failures" that reinforces the analysis paralysis.

- *The truth:* The Analyzer thinks they're being wise, but

wisdom requires movement, not just thought. Clarity doesn't come from endless thinking—it comes from action, feedback, and lived experience. The path doesn't get revealed through logic alone—it unfolds through trust.

THE COMPETITOR

- *What it looks like:* You measure your worth against others constantly. Every success is a comparison point, every achievement a scoreboard. You push yourself harder not because you're driven by joy—but because you're terrified of being left behind, overlooked, or seen as "less than."

- *What's underneath:* Fear of inadequacy. A belief that love, success, and attention are scarce resources. Deep conditioning that told you your value only comes from being better than someone else.

- *Core wound:* "If I'm not the best, I'm nothing."

- *Emotional roots:* Jealousy. Insecurity. Anxiety masked as ambition. A hidden grief that says, "Even when I win, it never feels like enough."

- *The truth:* The Competitor thrives in environments where external validation is currency. But true success isn't measured by beating others—it's measured by becoming more of yourself. When you stop running races you never wanted to be in, you start discovering what real fulfillment feels like.

THE CARETAKER

- *What it looks like:* You're the one everyone leans on. You anticipate needs before they're spoken, hold space for everyone's emotions, and pride yourself on being "the strong one." You rarely ask for help and feel guilty even thinking about putting yourself first.

- *What's underneath:* Fear of being a burden. A belief that your worth is tied to how useful you are to others. A subconscious strategy to gain love and safety through service.

- *Core wound:* "If I'm not needed, I'll be abandoned."

- *Emotional roots:* Guilt. Resentment. Suppressed grief. Chronic emotional fatigue masked as "being dependable."

- *The truth:* The Caretaker archetype is often born in environments where your needs were dismissed, but your caregiving was praised. Over time, giving became your identity. But constant caregiving without reciprocity leads to burnout and disconnection. True care includes yourself. You can't keep pouring from a cup you're not allowed to fill.

THE IMPOSTOR

- *What it looks like:* You're constantly waiting for the other shoe to drop—believing it's only a matter of time before people realize you're a fraud. No matter how much you've accomplished, you downplay it. You defer praise. You live with an internal sense of "Who am I supposed to be in this situation?" You over-prepare, over-explain, and over-apologize just to prove your worth.

- *What's underneath:* A deep-seated fear of being exposed as inadequate. You may have grown up in environments where success was either dismissed, over-criticized, or came with strings attached. You internalized the idea that if you shine too brightly, you'll be targeted—or worse, abandoned. So now, you try to earn your belonging by performing humility, minimizing your brilliance, and keeping the bar just out of reach.

- *Core wound:* "If they really knew me, they'd see I'm not enough."

- *Emotional roots:* Insecurity. Fear of rejection. Inner conflict between desire and deserving. The impostor carries grief around their true self never feeling quite safe to be seen. There's also a heavy dose of self-abandonment—of muting your gifts, softening your edges, and questioning your success so you can stay "safe" in the crowd.

- *The truth:* You're not an impostor. You're just expanding into an identity that your nervous system isn't used to yet. Impostor syndrome is a sign that you're stepping outside your old programming, not that you don't belong. Your success is real. Your gifts are needed. And you don't have to wait for permission to take up space. You were made for this. All of it.

THE INVISIBLE ONE

- *What it looks like:* You shrink in rooms, hold back your opinions, and avoid the spotlight at all costs. You might be the one who never speaks up in meetings, never posts about your wins, and automatically defers to others. When attention does come your way, you feel uncomfortable or even guilty. You blend in. You stay small. You make yourself easy to overlook—even when part of you is dying to be seen.

- *What's underneath:* A learned belief that visibility equals danger. Maybe as a child, being seen meant being punished, ridiculed, or burdened with expectations you weren't ready for. Maybe your needs were ignored until you learned it was safer not to have any. You equated safety with invisibility. Now, you associate being seen with exposure, judgment, or the possibility of getting it wrong.

- *Core wound:* "If I'm visible, I'll be judged, hurt, or abandoned."

- *Emotional roots:* Fear. Grief. Chronic self-doubt. Emo-

tional numbness. A sense of futility around being noticed or celebrated. Often there's a long history of
emotional neglect—either from others or internalized
self-neglect—that taught you your presence didn't matter. So you keep hiding, hoping someone will finally notice, but too afraid to step forward on your own.

- *The truth:* You were never meant to disappear. Your presence matters. Your voice matters. The world doesn't need
  another muted version of you—it needs the fully expressed, fully alive you. Visibility is not a threat; it's a
  right. And you don't have to earn it through perfection
  or performance. You were born to be seen—exactly as
  you are.

THE DRAMA SEEKER

- *What it looks like:* You're always in the middle of
  chaos—whether it's yours or someone else's. There's always a crisis, a conflict, or some emotional storm brew-
  ing. You might bounce from one high-stakes situation to
  the next, attract turbulent relationships, or create tension where there was peace. Drama feels like fuel. When
  things get quiet or calm, you get restless—or even anxious.

- *What's underneath:* A nervous system wired for chaos.
  Drama can be a cover for deeper emotional needs—like
  wanting attention, connection, or validation—but not
  knowing how to ask for them directly. It's also often a

way to avoid the discomfort of stillness, where you might have to face boredom, emptiness, or long-buried pain. You may have grown up in an environment where drama was the norm, so now chaos feels like home—even when it hurts.

- *Core wound:* "If there's no drama, there's no connection or meaning."

- *Emotional roots:* Anxiety. Abandonment fear. Emotional intensity as a survival mechanism. Often rooted in childhood dynamics where calm equaled disconnection or invisibility, and only crisis brought attention or closeness. There may also be a subconscious belief that peace is boring or that happiness is too good to last.

- *The truth:* You don't need chaos to be important. You don't need intensity to be alive. Peace doesn't mean nothing is happening—it means something deeper can finally emerge. Stillness is where healing lives. Drama is a habit, not your identity. You're allowed to choose calm, ease, and grounded joy without waiting for the next explosion to prove you're still here.

THE OUTSIDER

- *What it looks like:* You walk into rooms already assuming you don't belong. You keep yourself slightly removed—from groups, conversations, communities, even relationships. You're observant, self-reliant, and maybe even proud of your ability to stay on the fringes. You tell yourself you don't need anyone, or that no one really "gets" you. You're often the lone wolf, the wall-flower, or the one who ghosts before things get too close.

- *What's underneath:* A fear of rejection masked as de-tachment. The Outsider learned early on that inclu-sion came at a cost—maybe it meant being judged, hurt, or made to conform. So you built your safety in solitude. Belonging became suspicious. You convinced yourself that staying separate was strength, but really it's a shield—protecting you from the vulnerability of being truly seen.

- *Core wound:* "If I get too close, I'll be rejected—or worse, I'll lose myself."

- *Emotional roots:* Loneliness. Fear of abandonment. Identity confusion. Often tied to experiences of being left out, misunderstood, or labeled "different" as a child. There may be trauma around feeling excluded or be-trayed by the very people you tried to connect with.

- *The truth:* You do belong—exactly as you are. You don't have to shrink, morph, or perform to be included. The right people will meet you in your wholeness, not your performance. Connection doesn't have to cost you your individuality. Being seen is scary, yes—but it's also where the healing begins. You're not too different. You're deeply needed—just not by everyone. And that's okay.

THE ADDICT

- *What it looks like:* You latch onto something—substances, food, work, love, chaos, scrolling, drama—and you go all in. It consumes your thoughts, your time, your energy. Maybe it looks "functional" on the outside, but underneath, you know it's a coping mechanism. You use it to escape, to soothe, to numb, or to fill a void that nothing ever quite seems to reach.

- *What's underneath:* A profound ache for relief. The Addict isn't reckless—they're resourceful. It's the part of you that figured out how to survive unbearable emotional pain by finding something, anything, to take the edge off. This archetype usually forms around deep emotional wounds, where feelings were overwhelming, dismissed, or outright unsafe. Addiction becomes a relationship—reliable, predictable, always there when people or reality aren't.

- *Core wound:* "I can't be with what I feel—it's too much."

- *Emotional roots:* Shame. Grief. Emotional abandonment. Often tied to childhood experiences of neglect, chaos, trauma, or having no one who could help you regulate. The Addict is born when emotional overwhelm has no healthy outlet, and soothing must be sourced elsewhere—externally, urgently, and repetitively.

- *The truth:* You are not broken, weak, or beyond help.

You are someone who developed brilliant survival tools in the absence of safety. But those tools are now costing you your aliveness. The real healing isn't in fighting the addiction—it's in meeting the wound underneath it. You don't have to numb to be okay. You can learn to feel and stay. You can build capacity. You can let go of the crutch and find connection—first with yourself, then with others. You're not too much. You were just left to hold too much, alone.

THE PERPETUAL STUDENT

- *What it looks like:* You're always learning, always enrolling in another course, reading the next book, getting yet another certification. You have notebooks full of insights, folders of PDFs, podcasts queued up for days. But when it comes time to actually do the thing? You hesitate. You freeze. You convince yourself you just need to learn one more thing first.

- *What's underneath:* Fear of inadequacy. Fear of exposure. A belief that you'll never be "ready enough" or "expert enough" to take action. Knowledge becomes a shield—if you just know enough, you can avoid judgment, failure, or criticism. But that same shield keeps you stuck, always preparing, never leaping.

- *Core wound:* "If I take action and fail, it'll prove I'm not enough."

- *Emotional roots:* Insecurity. Fear of being seen. Fear of being wrong or humiliated. Often tied to childhood experiences of being shamed for not knowing something, or praised only for being "the smart one." The Perpetual Student often carries perfectionist tendencies masked as curiosity.

- *The truth:* You already know enough to begin. Embodiment is the missing piece. Information without integration is just another flavor of avoidance. Learning is beautiful, but it's meant to empower—not imprison. You don't need another credential to be worthy. You need courage to trust what's already within you. Start before you're ready. That's where the real learning lives.

THE GATEKEEPER

- *What it looks like:* You keep yourself under lock and key—emotionally, creatively, and energetically. You might have a lot to offer, but you only share pieces of yourself after extreme vetting. You hold back your truth, your magic, your desires... waiting for the perfect time, the perfect safety, or the perfect person who "deserves" to see you. Even then, it's only ever a controlled glimpse.

- *What's underneath:* Fear of vulnerability. Fear of being misunderstood, judged, or rejected. A belief that being fully seen is dangerous—that openness equals exposure, and exposure leads to pain. The Gatekeeper learned early that privacy was protection, and expression had consequences.

- *Core wound:* "If I let them see the real me, they'll use it against me."

- *Emotional roots:* Distrust. Hypervigilance. Emotional self-protection. Often rooted in betrayal, emotional neglect, or past experiences of having your openness weaponized against you. The Gatekeeper is often mistaken for being guarded or aloof, when in reality, they're deeply sensitive and fiercely protective of their truth.

- *The truth:* You don't have to fling the doors wide open to be free. But living with every door locked is its own kind of prison. You can start by letting yourself in. By allowing your truth to exist without performance or permission. The right people don't need you to hand over the keys all at once—they just need to feel your presence. Your power isn't in what you hide. It's in what you're willing to own, even quietly, even gently, even if it's just for you. Safety isn't built through isolation. It's built through discernment, boundaries, and radical self-trust.

THE CRITICALLY ENLIGHTENED

- *What it looks like:* You've done the work. You've read the books, gone to the workshops, collected certifications like Girl Scout badges. You can quote Jung, Dispenza, and Byron Katie in your sleep. You dissect patterns, spot projections, and coach yourself mid-breakdown.

You know why you do what you do—but nothing seems to change. Because here's the catch: insight has become armor. You're so in your head, analyzing every trigger and reaction, that you've disconnected from your body, your intuition, and your raw, unfiltered truth.

- *What's underneath:* Fear of vulnerability. Fear of chaos. A need for control masquerading as mastery. A belief that understanding equals healing—and if you can just intellectualize it enough, you won't have to feel it.

- *Core wound:* "If I understand it all, I can stay safe."

- *Emotional roots:* Over-intellectualization. Emotional by-passing. Deep discomfort with the messiness of emotion and embodiment. Often rooted in environments where emotional expression was punished, shamed, or ignored—so thinking became the safest place to live.

- *The truth:* Wisdom is beautiful. But insight without embodiment is just noise. You don't heal by knowing—you heal by feeling, integrating, and showing up differently. You can't out-think your shadow. You can't strategize your way into softness. Your next level of transformation won't come from another book or breakthrough—it'll come from letting go of the need to always have it "figured out." You don't need more theory. You need more truth, more tenderness, and more trust in your own heart.

Each of these voices has a root. A moment. A memory. A belief. And yes, once upon a time, they helped you survive. But now? They're boxing you in.

By now, you are probably thinking you are soooo far gone. You see that you have just about every single one of those archetypes in you. Don't spiral out. You are fine. It is normal to see each or at least most of those within yourself. It doesn't mean that you are that messed up. Everyone should see some of these inside or maybe have shown them at one time or another in their life. Remember, it is when you see them as being your go-to programming that it could be an issue for you. And hey, if one or more of the above archetypes are working for you, then fantastic. You do you, boo. But for those that have seen these as being a barrier to getting what you truly want, continue your reading here.

Sabotage isn't just something you do. It's something you become—until you realize you don't have to anymore.

This is why shadow work matters. Mindset work scratches the surface, but your nervous system doesn't speak affirmation. It speaks emotion. Energy. Embodiment. That's why "thinking positive" alone doesn't shift patterns that are wired in survival. You have to dig deeper. You have to meet those inner parts with truth, not just talk.

As Byron Katie says, "We don't question what we don't see." So start seeing it. Let the pattern show itself. Get curious, not cruel.

Carolyn Elliott challenges us to ask what part of us enjoys the sabotage. What twisted sense of familiarity or control does it give us? This isn't about blame. It's about honesty. Radical, liberating honesty.

Let's call it what it is: sabotage is strategy. A strategy that's outdated, overused, and ready to be retired.

But first, it needs to be named. Seen. Acknowledged.

Because you can't heal what you're still pretending isn't there.

Where It Starts: Shadow Work & Jung's Big Truth

Carl Jung was a badass. He was the first to tell us what many of us already felt but didn't have words for:

> "UNTIL YOU MAKE THE UNCONSCIOUS CON-
> SCIOUS, IT WILL DIRECT YOUR LIFE AND YOU
> WILL CALL IT FATE."

Let's talk about the shadow for a second—not the creepy figure lurking behind you, but the parts of your psyche you've disowned, denied, or shoved down so deep you forgot they were even there.

Your shadow isn't just the ugly stuff. It's your brilliance, your sensuality, your rage, your boundaries, your power. It's everything you learned to hide in order to belong.

Here's the kicker: **your sabotage is often run by your shadow.** That disowned part of you that got the message (usually in childhood) that it wasn't safe to be big, loud, angry, soft, honest, vulnerable, too smart, too pretty, too ambitious, too sensitive, too much... or not enough.

So instead of embodying your full self, you built a persona that was acceptable. You played the good girl. The responsible one. The overachiever. The martyr. The "easy" one. And those masks? They worked. Until they didn't.

Shadow work is the process of peeling back those layers—not to become someone new, but to remember who you were before the world told you to tone it down. It's confronting the old wounds and beliefs that shaped your survival strategy. It's noticing the parts of yourself you're ashamed of and asking: "Who told me this wasn't allowed?"

You want freedom? This is where it starts. Not with hustle. Not with more self-help books or motivational quotes. With presence. With curiosity. With the willingness to meet your shadow in the dark and say, "Okay, I see you."

Here's what shadow work isn't: it's not about shame-dumping, spiraling in pain, or getting lost in trauma porn. It's about truth. Integration. Wholeness.

Because the parts you repress don't go away. They fester. They sabotage. They control your choices from behind the curtain. But when you bring them to light—when you stop judging them and start listening—they become allies. Fierce ones.

So yes, the shadow is scary. But it's also sacred. It's the portal to your most unapologetic self. And when you start doing this work, things shift. Not because you've "fixed" yourself—but because you finally stopped abandoning yourself.

However, this is where I see so many people getting stuck in the cycle. Shadow work works but only if you come up for air long enough to enjoy life around you. Enlightened ones, lost souls, and honestly-trying-to-do-the-work all have found themselves on this endless merry-go-round of shadows to integrate. You can get lost in the depths of your inner child, trying to acknowledge and accept every single shadow you have. I am here to say that you don't need to take this plunge into your own abyss, sifting every layer to see some major changes in your current life. Nor do I promote this in my coaching. Pick one at a time to explore and work with. Then, come back up to the surface.

The Dark Secret: Sometimes You Like the Sabotage

Enter: Carolyn Elliott and *Existential Kink*.

If you haven't read this gem, here's the mic-drop summary: **there's a part of you that secretly enjoys the very crap you say you want to escape.**

Ouch. I know. But stay with me.

This isn't about blaming yourself. It's about getting radically honest. There's often a sneaky sense of *safety* or even pleasure in staying stuck. And it's not because you're broken or masochistic—it's because some part of you learned to associate suffering with control. Familiar pain is still familiar. It's predictable. And predictability, to your nervous system, feels like safety.

Staying small means you don't have to face criticism. You don't have to prove yourself. You don't have to risk being exposed or misunderstood.

Playing poor means you never have to navigate complicated money dynamics or the discomfort of others' envy. You get to stay in the identity you've built—humble, struggling, relatable.

Being overwhelmed means no one can expect more from you. It justifies the delay. The pass. The flake. The burnout becomes a badge of honor.

Sabotaging relationships means you don't have to risk real intimacy, vulnerability, or heartbreak. You get to stay independent, in control, emotionally armored.

Carolyn calls this the "kink"—the unconscious part of you that *gets off* on the dysfunction. The twist is that you don't even realize you're doing it. But once you do, it's like turning on a light in a room you've been fumbling around in for decades.

And when you bring that kink to the light—when you own it without shame or guilt—you get your power back.

Because what you can own, you can shift.

There's something almost rebellious about admitting, "Yeah, part of me *likes* this drama. This chaos. This failure loop. It keeps me in control. It keeps me safe. It lets me feel something." That honesty? That's your gateway to freedom. You can't change what you're still pretending you don't choose.

Radical ownership isn't self-blame. It's sovereignty.

This work invites you to turn toward your patterns with compassion and curiosity, not judgment. Ask yourself, "What am I getting out of this? What does this pattern protect me from? What does it give me that I'm not getting elsewhere?"

Because when you admit you like the sabotage—even a little—you stop being its victim. You become its witness. And then? You become its alchemist.

We'll come back to this. As we move through this process, you'll see how naming the kink, the shadow, and the sabotage isn't where it ends—it's where it *begins*. This isn't about staying in the dark. It's about using what we uncover here to transmute pain into power. We're not here to romanticize the wreckage—we're here to rise from it. When we shift from shadow into light, it's not about bypassing the dark. It's about integrating it so it no longer runs the show. More on that soon.

The Beliefs That Built the Cage

Now let's talk about limiting beliefs. Not the cute little ones you can shake off with an affirmation, but the sticky, deep-seated kind that wrap themselves around your decisions, your identity, and your sense of possibility like a boa constrictor in slow motion.

Here's where we flip the script a bit. A lot of traditional self-help models will tell you that it all starts with thoughts. "Change your thoughts, change your life," right? But if you've ever tried that and still felt stuck, here's why:

It doesn't start with thoughts. It starts with **emotions**. While traditional cognitive models start with thought → emotion → behavior, a more body-based or energetic approach recognizes that **emotions often precede thoughts**, especially when they're rooted in unresolved experiences or trauma.

Here's the real loop:

Emotion → Thought → Action → Result → Belief.

Let that sink in.

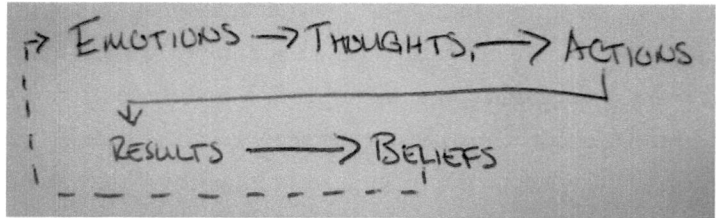

You have a feeling—maybe it's fear, shame, grief, or even excitement—and your mind rushes in to make meaning out of it. That's where the thought forms. The thought triggers an action—or inaction. That action leads to a result. And after enough repetition, that result turns into a belief. Boom. That belief then acts like a silent operating system, influencing how you show up in every damn area of your life.

And the kicker? It all started with an emotion. Not logic. Not reason. Just raw, unfiltered emotion.

These beliefs sound like:

"IF I'M TOO SUCCESSFUL, PEOPLE WILL RESENT ME."
"IF I REST, I'M LAZY."
"IF I'M NOT PERFECT, I'LL BE REJECTED."
"IF I SPEAK UP, I'LL BE PUNISHED."
"IF I FAIL, I'LL LOSE EVERYTHING."

They sound like truth. But they're not.

They're echoes of past experiences—what you saw, felt, or were told as a child. They were passed down through family systems, cultural expectations, religious messaging, and lived experiences. They weren't your conscious choices. They were your conditioning.

And yet, they build the walls of the cage you now live in.

Here's where Byron Katie's work in *Loving What Is* becomes a wrecking ball:

1. Is it true?

2. Can I absolutely know that it's true?

3. How do I react when I believe that thought?

4. Who would I be without that thought?

This is where the excavation begins. Not with blame. Not with shame. But with curiosity.

Because when you can start tracing those results back to your actions, those actions back to your thoughts, and those thoughts back to your emotions—you find the root. And when you find the root, you can dig it the hell up.

You can't mindset your way out of something that was built on emotional wiring. You have to go there. To the messy, uncomfortable, powerful realm of the emotional body. That's where the real rewiring begins.

And the truth? You don't need to burn it all down to build something new. You just need to become aware. Because once you see the loop, you can start interrupting it. One emotion. One thought. One action at a time.

Welcome to the real work.

Why You Keep Repeating the Same Patterns

Back to the body for a second. Because sabotage isn't just mental—it's embodied. It lives in your cells. In your muscle memory. In the energy that vibrates beneath your skin like a low hum of old stories.

As Dr. Joe Dispenza puts it, your body becomes addicted to the chemical cocktail of your past. Every emotion you've felt repeatedly—fear, shame, disappointment, grief—releases a unique blend of neurochemicals. And over time, those chemicals become familiar. Comfortable, even. Your body begins to crave them like a smoker craves nicotine. Not because they feel good, but because they feel known.

So even if your conscious mind says, "Yes, let's go after joy, love, expansion," your body says, "Hold the fuck up—this isn't what we know. This feels dangerous."

And what happens next?

Your body revolts. Literally. Your heart races. Your stomach knots. Your breath shortens. Your nervous system sounds the alarm bells.

And your brain, ever the loyal meaning-maker, scrambles to justify the panic:

"MAYBE I CAN'T AFFORD THIS."
"MAYBE THEY DON'T REALLY LIKE ME."
"MAYBE I'M NOT READY."
"MAYBE IT'S SAFER TO WAIT."

These thoughts aren't random. They're your nervous system trying to pull you back to the emotional baseline you've been living in for years—decades, even. That baseline might be fear, loneliness, overwhelm, or even lack. But it's *yours*. It's familiar. And familiar equals safe to the primal brain.

So you sabotage. Not because you're broken. But because your nervous system doesn't yet believe it's safe to have what you're reaching for. The joy, the love, the success, the peace—all of it can feel foreign, and therefore, threatening.

This is why people repeat the same patterns over and over again. Not because they aren't smart or strong or spiritual enough. But because their body is fighting for homeostasis in a system that was wired in survival.

You can have the dream on your vision board, the mantra on your mirror, the plan in your journal—but if your body still believes that joy equals danger, you'll unconsciously sabotage to protect yourself from that perceived threat.

This is why nervous system regulation and emotional integration are so important. You don't just need mindset shifts. You need body trust. You need to teach your system that it's safe to feel good. Safe to expand. Safe to live beyond survival.

Otherwise, the loop continues. And you call it fate.

But it's not fate. It's programming. And you, my peep, are allowed to rewrite it.

Sabotage as a Comfort Zone Ritual

Let's be real. You know the pattern.

- YOU GET INSPIRED. BIG IDEA. VISION BOARD. CLEAN NOTEBOOK.

- YOU TAKE THE FIRST STEP.

- SOMETHING GOES WRONG. YOU FREAK OUT.

- YOU TALK YOURSELF OUT OF IT.

- YOU BINGE-WATCH SCHITT'S CREEK AND SCROLL ZILLOW LIKE IT'S YOUR JOB.

- YOU FEEL LIKE CRAP.

- YOU BLAME YOURSELF.

- YOU MAKE A NEW PLAN.

- REPEAT.

That's not laziness. That's the ritual of sabotage. And it's not your fault. But it is your responsibility to change it.

See, sabotage becomes a ritual because it's familiar. Predictable. Weirdly comforting. It's a self-fulfilling prophecy that reinforces the belief, "See? This is why I never follow through." But the truth is, this ritual is less about your motivation and more about your nervous system trying to stay within its window of what feels emotionally safe.

You might even catch yourself feeling weird when things are *going well*. You'll manufacture stress, pick a fight, or delay the good just long enough to feel normal again. That's not random. That's your body trying to return to its baseline. To the emotional frequency it knows—whether that's anxiety, chaos, struggle, or disappointment.

We romanticize the hustle, the comeback, the redemption arc. But we rarely acknowledge the part where we sabotage so we *can* come back. Where we knock ourselves off the pedestal just so we can earn our way back up. It's dramatic, exhausting, and very on-brand for sabotage.

Comfort zone rituals are sneaky. They'll convince you you're being "realistic," or "humble," or "careful." But what they're really doing is keeping you small, looping you in a cycle that makes you feel safe in stagnation.

I know this all too well in my personal life. It can even happen with a project that I have been making headway with. I have found myself taking a day to rest because I was all "gung-ho" for the past 4 days...only to have completed the whole season 3 of *Ginny & Georgia*. True story. I spent 3 days taking a "self-care" moment. But then to get myself back into it, I may need a stick of dynamite. While my eyes were fixed on the television screen, my mind was spinning out with hurtful thoughts, sinking emotions, and even some not so healthy food choices. Luckily, I can recognize this as a pattern of mine.

So the next time you find yourself retreating from progress, ask yourself: What part of me feels unsafe in expansion? What old pattern am I reenacting here? Because the cycle will keep spinning as long as it goes unchecked.

You're not a victim of your patterns. You're the one running them. Which means you're the one who can rewrite them. And rewriting starts with awareness. Then repetition. Then radical rebellion against the script that says you're only allowed to want something if you're willing to suffer for it.

You get to break the loop. You get to build new rituals that feel like freedom, not fear. And you get to do it now. Because the more you learn to recognize the shape of your sabotage, the quicker you'll be able to shift out of it before it hijacks your entire damn week (or month... or life).

I want to take a moment here and highlight something to you. Moments ago, I shared how I was able to binge watch the whole third season of *Ginny & Georgia*. If you are reading this in 2025, then you will know that this season is *new*. That's right. I recently have been stuck in my comfort zone of sabotage, spiralling out. This is not because the process is not working. It's because I have 31 years of outdated programming I am working through. The steps may sound easy but the process is a multi-layered puzzle and even though you have been making leaps and bounds in your life, you will find yourself from time to time with a new exciting layer to work with.

I love the saying, "Rome wasn't built in a day." Neither were you. We are having to tear down some of the old structures you are accustomed to in order to make space to build the new. This takes time. So please, give yourself a bit of grace.

So What Do You Do With All This?

First, breathe.

Seriously. Take a breath.

You're not crazy. You're not a failure. You're not broken. And you're definitely not the only one dealing with this. You're waking up. That's it. You're waking up to the invisible systems that have been running the show in the background—unseen, unchallenged, but deeply influential. And once you see them, you can't unsee them. That's the gift. That's the ache. That's the beginning.

But let's get one thing straight: you don't need to fix it all right now. You don't need to cleanse your whole life like it's Mercury retrograde in Scorpio. You don't need to earn your healing or hustle for your worth.

This isn't about flipping your life upside down. It's about gently turning the volume down on your inner chaos long enough to hear the truth underneath. And that truth sounds like:

You are not your patterns.

You are not your worst moment.

You are not defined by what you've survived.

What you *are* is powerful. Capable. And ready—even if you don't feel like it.

Here's the simplest place to begin:

Awareness + Willingness = Momentum.

Awareness of the pattern. Willingness to look at it with honesty. Momentum to start shifting it with small, doable choices.

You don't need a 40-step healing blueprint. You need presence. Curiosity. Tiny acts of rebellion against the old programming.

Nervous system support. Energetic clearing. Conscious breath. A journal. Maybe a mirror. And for sure, a deep belly laugh.

This work is sacred, yes—but it's also messy and mundane and wildly human. Some days it will look like breakthroughs. Other days it'll look like remembering to drink water and go outside.

And humor—don't forget that. Sometimes healing sounds like, "Oh, damn... I do that. Huh." Sometimes it's laughing until you cry at how absurdly human this whole thing is. Sometimes it's screaming into a pillow, then making a snack and texting your weirdest friend. There's no "right" way to heal. There's just *your* way. One real, imperfect, radically honest step at a time.

Let's dig deeper next chapter. Because naming the sabotage/shadow is step one. Unhooking from it? That's where the real magic begins.

Four

SUBCONSCIOUS TRUTH-TELLING

Here's where we make the shift. Now that you have all of the knowledge about what has been happening behind the curtains. The wizard is now fully exposed and you can now make the shift to who you really want to be. Who you were meant to be.

From here on out, I will be sharing with you the steps I use in my coaching program MindShift. Each step of the way, you will be able to learn more about yourself and put into action what you need to so you can manifest the life you want to create.

This is the work of subconscious truth-telling: not just identifying your sabotage or analyzing your past, but listening to what your body, your energy, and your emotional landscape are trying to say underneath it all. We need to dive deep in order to rise up.

I have already discussed how many people will get stuck in the deep dive of shadow work and integrating it as well as the sabotage into their life. So many people can get lost here, sometimes for years. I want to also take this time to share that in my practice, I have found many people are kept in one of three areas of this enlightenment process: the exploration of sabotage and the shadow, the flipping of the frequency of emotions, or the manifestation phase.

Shadow exploration brings awareness to your wounds and defense mechanisms. Emotional frequency work raises your state so you can attract new experiences. Manifestation practices focus on aligning with what you want. But here's the thing—if your energy field is still cluttered with unresolved blockages, you're building on a shaky foundation. That's why the fourth pillar, energetic clearing, is essential. It's the bridge between insight and embodiment. Between knowing and becoming.

Each of these three areas can produce some real change, however, I see them all falling short of continued growth because we are still not rewiring our operating system. It is through the practice of all three sections, as well as the inclusion of that fourth part, that we can have lasting results.

Before we dive head first into our personal shadow and sabotaging beliefs, I want to make a quick statement. This part of the journey will require you to take a step back from your ego and let go of your logical mind. I have seen so many shadow work journals out there on the market claiming they have the perfect prompts for you to unlock the shadow and integrate it back into the light. However, I hate...okay maybe not hate, that is a bit strong. But I really have a bad taste in my mouth for journal prompt workbooks. They keep you locked in the left brain with its question/answer format. You are kept in the logical mind and never really get to step into the subconscious mind, your inner wisdom and voice.

The subconscious doesn't speak in bullet points or tidy answers. It speaks in metaphor. In resistance. In gut feelings and sudden memories. Linear questions can only take you so far. If you're only answering what you think you *should* say, you're not doing shadow work—you're doing PR for your inner child. This is about letting the messy, wild, unfiltered truth come forward.

Meditation is great. It allows you to tap into this part of your being where secrets are held. However, if you are like me, then as soon as you come back to the earthly plane, you lose over half of the information. Also, if you try to write notes as you meditate, then you are having to tap in and out of the meditation process, only making it so much longer and increasing the chances of you walking right back into your left brain again.

If shadow work journals work for you, great. If meditation works, perfect. You do you, boo. However, I will be using my process to getting deep into your inner brain. So if you are ready to take that closer look as to what the fuck is happening inside, buckle up. We are about to head down the tarmac.

This is where the rubber meets the soul. You're not here to play nice with your patterns anymore. You're here to pull back the curtain, dig in, and finally meet the parts of yourself you've been both avoiding and aching to understand. We're not talking about surface-level awareness. We're going to the source.

Hint. Hint: This is the time to grab a pen and a blank paper journal.

The First Thread

Let's start simple—but not small.

Choose one thing. One sticky pattern, one invisible wall, one area where your wheels keep spinning. It could be something external like a career move you keep procrastinating on or a financial threshold you can't seem to surpass. Or maybe it's internal—a sense of never being "enough," a fear of being seen, a low-grade hum of anxiety that shows up every time you try to rest.

The key is this: **it needs to feel emotionally charged.** You don't need to have a solution. You don't even need to fully understand it yet. You just need to feel the pull—the tension between what you want and where you are.

Write it down. Get honest. Get specific. "I want to stop undercharging my clients." "I want to break the pattern of dating emotionally unavailable people." "I want to feel confident enough to speak up at work." Don't fluff it up or try to make it sound good. The more raw and real it is, the more power it holds. Maybe you don't really know what you want specifically. Maybe you just know that you want to have a better relationship or feel more fulfilled in your career or start a new business or even want to increase the digits in your bank account or lose that weight once and for all.

And let's be clear: this isn't about setting a neat, motivational goal. This is about calling your subconscious to the table. It's about pulling the thread that leads to the deeper weave—the beliefs, stories, and energies that are keeping you looped in the same outcomes.

Think of this as your *invocation*. You're not begging for change. You're demanding clarity. You're letting your system know, "Hey,

I'm ready to look." And that simple act of choosing—of naming the friction point without trying to fix it—is wildly powerful.

Why? Because most people don't stop to name what's actually running the show. They try to set surface goals while their subconscious is still clutching onto old fears and identities. But when you pause and say, "This is the loop I'm ready to face," your inner world listens. The shadows stir. The patterns perk up. Your energy starts to shift—not because you've solved it, but because you've finally seen it.

So grab your journal, and let's begin with this intention:

"I'M WILLING TO SEE WHAT'S BEEN DRIVING THIS PATTERN. I'M READY TO MEET WHAT I'VE BEEN AVOIDING."

From there, the path starts to reveal itself.

Notes to ponder

A little note here...you might have a slew of things you want to change in your current life and that is okay. Write them all down. But for this work, we will only focus on one. As the work goes on, you may notice that other areas of your life will begin to shift as well. I always think it is fun to see how doing deep centered work can impact several areas of your life, even when you are really only immersed in one.

Okay...second note. This one of caution. As you begin this work, you may find that life will throw you a curveball. Life's changeup is an energetic means to throw you off track and knock you off your pedestal. You may have already seen this as you picked up this book and decided to read it. Why? **Disruption follows decision.**

As soon as you make a decision to make a change. To try something new, life is going to step in and derail you. You may have a family member enter the hospital. Work calls you for extra shifts, pulling you away from what you were wanting to do.

I had a client get sick immediately after starting her 8-week program to shift her life. We both laughed at it as we had just discussed this very thing in the group session earlier in the week. It was as though the universe heard her say, "I want better in my life and I am going to do whatever it takes to get there." The universe responded with a whammy, trying to keep her in her comfort zone. I am not talking like she had the sniffles. She was laid out for about a week and had even thought about going to the urgent care because it came out of nowhere, straight out of left field.

How do you combat this? Get ready for it. Really, that is about all you can do. Make sure you have a solid support system around you, keeping you going if needed. Remind yourself...once it hits, it means you are onto something big. Something bold. If you need to take a moment to take care of the immediate issue, do such, but then saddle back up and get on that horse once again. Don't let life or the universe shake you loose from your goal.

Let the Shadow Speak: The Power of a 10-Minute Freewrite

So you've named the thing. That sticky-ass pattern. The block that keeps showing up like a bad sequel. Now it's time to crack it open.

We're not doing this with logic, strategy, or another color-coded action plan. We're doing it by dropping into your subconscious—fast, raw, and real. That's where the truth is hiding. That's where the power is.

This is where we begin what I call the **10-Minute Freewrite**.

Now, before your inner overachiever tries to make this cute or polished, let me stop you right there. This is not a journal prompt. This is not a gratitude list. This is you giving your inner world the mic for ten uninterrupted minutes. No censoring. No editing. No trying to sound like a self-aware wellness goddess on Instagram.

This is where your shadow gets to speak. Unfiltered. Messy. Maybe even a little mean. And that's the point.

What Is a Freewrite?

A freewrite is a stream-of-consciousness writing practice where you put pen to paper (or fingers to keys) and don't stop for ten minutes. No correcting, no backspacing, no fixing your grammar (because of the auto correcting and ease of backspace, I actually highly recommend you do this work with paper and pen). You don't even have to make sense. You just let the thoughts flow—especially the weird, uncomfortable, or "ugly" ones you normally shove aside.

Your job is not to control it. Your job is to let the words fall out.

Start with the thing you identified in the last section—your goal, your block, your sticky loop. Write it at the top of your page. Then, hit go. We want to see what your thoughts are behind the area you are wanting to shift. If you are wanting to make more money, you don't want to ask you subconscious "How can I make more money?" We are interested in your thoughts, feels, and hidden secrets circling around money.

Let whatever thoughts, emotions, fears, or stories surface. Even if they seem petty, dramatic, or totally irrational.

"THIS FEELS STUPID."

"MY HAND IS CRAMPING."

"I ALWAYS MESS THIS UP."

"WHAT IF PEOPLE LAUGH AT ME?"

"I KNOW I'M CAPABLE BUT I DON'T FEEL IT."

"I WANT TO CHANGE BUT I ALSO KINDA DON'T."

That last one? Gold. That's your shadow talking. That's what we're here for.

If it is a thought in you head, then it needs to go onto the paper. From head, to hand, to paper. And remember...no censoring.

WHY IT WORKS

Your logical mind—your left brain—is excellent at problem-solving, but it's also a gatekeeper. It filters, judges, and edits your inner experience. It wants everything to make sense, to be socially acceptable, to sound "right."

But your truth? It doesn't live in the polished part of you. It lives in the raw, murky, emotionally charged center. That's the subconscious. And the only way to access it is to stop performing and start allowing.

Free writing bypasses the ego's filters. It allows your deeper self to rise to the surface without getting interrupted by fear or shame. Think of it like opening a hidden channel in your mind—and letting your emotional body dictate the signal.

Most of us spend so much time trying to "figure it out" from the top down—logically diagnosing ourselves like we're broken software. But your patterns, your sabotage, your resistance? They don't need to be analyzed. They need to be witnessed.

How to Do It

Set a timer for 10 minutes.

Not 5. Not 3. Give yourself the full 10 minutes. It takes time for your conscious mind to step aside and your subconscious to step forward. Just like with fascia releasing, you will see that at about minute 3, your subconscious will kick in and take over. Like the well-used muscle it is, the brain will relax and release after 3 minutes. Until then, you will be battling the left brain a bit. Just keep writing.

Why not 15 or 20 minutes then? Well, after that 10-minute mark, your brain will start to wander down other rabbit holes. You may shift to some answers on how to change your dilemma or your brain may try to organize it all for you. We do not need those answers. Even though "fixing" and organizing your thoughts sounds tempting, they will only keep you stuck. The freewrite becomes more of a task after about 10 minutes and your left, logical brain will love that. It will begin the whole thing as a "step-by-step mini project", locking you once again in the conscious side of things. Ten minutes is the sweet spot.

Write your focus phrase at the top.

This can be your goal, fear, pattern, or block. Keep it simple. Even just writing one word like "money" at the top of your page will work (as long as it is a financial thing you are wanting to work on). Remember, we are wanting your thoughts on the topic not a grocery list of how to fix it.

Start writing—and don't stop.

Even if you don't know what to say, write "I don't know what to say" until something else comes. Keep the pen moving. If you cry, fine. If you curse, great. If it feels repetitive, go with it. Repetition often reveals the core wound. If your hand is cramping? Write it down.

This is not a list. I want you to write this in paragraph format. Lists are a left brain dream date. There are plenty of stops and starts to go around so the brain can go all Type A on it and keep it pretty. Not what we want. So...write it out with sentences, not listing it.

Don't worry about legibility or grammar.

You're not writing a novel. You're excavating emotion. Sloppy handwriting and curse words are welcome here. In fact, you can find some hidden gems as you look over your freewrite based on how your handwriting looks or how hard you are pressing into the paper. Tuck that one away for the next step. Wink.

Let it get weird. Let it get honest.

This is sacred space. No one is reading this. You get to be as messy, raw, selfish, angry, or afraid as you need to be. Don't edit yourself. If you want real change, real answers...then let that freak flag fly.

THINGS THAT MIGHT COME UP (GOOD—LET THEM)

SHAME

CHILDHOOD FLASHBACKS

RANDOM THOUGHTS ABOUT YOUR EX OR YOUR MOM

RAGE OR BLAME

"THIS IS ALL POINTLESS" LOOPS

VISCERAL FEELINGS IN YOUR BODY

IMAGERY OR METAPHORS THAT SURPRISE YOU

Write it all. Because you're not trying to "get it right." You're trying to let it out.

And here's the magic: once you do, you'll begin to see the shape of your shadow. You'll see the stories that are holding the pattern in place. The hidden fears. The unmet needs. The shit you didn't know you still carried.

You can't shift what you refuse to see. This practice pulls back the curtain. It gets you out of the surface loop and into the real work. And no, it's not always fun. But it's always worth it.

So go now. Set your timer. Let the ink flow. You're not writing to impress. You're writing to uncover. And when the 10 minutes are up—then we'll look at what you found.

The Takeaways: Turning Thought into Truth

Now that you've let your shadow speak through the uncensored free write, it's time to sift through what emerged. This next step isn't about fixing anything—it's about getting radically honest with what your subconscious revealed. And one of the most powerful tools for doing this is Byron Katie's framework: *The Work*.

But first, let's comb through what you wrote down. I like doing this within a day or two of doing the free write. Anything longer and you may lose the vision and emotion for it. I don't recommend diving into it immediately afterwards as you are still coming down and need to now switch back into that left brain of yours. See...it's not a bad thing. Just not always what we need for healing.

As you read through this again, take a pen and underline or highlight key words or statements that stand out to you. Read this freewrite as if you are an investigator or therapist ready to ask more questions. What jumps out to you as main themes or breakthrough revolutions? Write these tidbits down on a separate page, leave some space between them so you can ask those investigative questions.

Let me share some of my own personal takeaways from my own practice I did a long time ago. This is a real, honest, raw look into how dark our inner selves can be. I pulled this straight out of my journal.

- Money is evil. Yet, I strive to have it.

  o Do I then see myself as evil or could I become evil if I have money?

- Being poor is a weakness.

  o Am I weak? Lazy? Hopeless? Worthless?

- I don't like to ask for help out of pride.

- I also run and hide when I fear being called out as poor because of the negative <u>image</u> I have of poor individuals.

  - Dirty, lazy, unhealthy, filthy, fleas, drugs, smell, thieves, cheap, clutter

- Money is power and gives you control.

  - Without money, am I out of control and have no power in my life?

- I have a very complicated relation-ship with money. Why? Love/Hate. And I still want to make fast, easy money.

- I don't want to be mean to others that have less than me. Robin Hood effect.

  - Is this why I don't have money?

- I don't deserve fast, easy, abundant money.

  - It wouldn't be earned or worked for.

Did you notice how I cut right into the dark abyss of my thoughts and feelings? This is not a Hallmark movie or an after-school special. This is junky, icky feeling work. You can easily see how complicated and tangled I was with the concept of money. So many conflicting thoughts holding me into a place where I could not go above my glass ceiling of financial wealth and on the other end, feeling ashamed if I dipped below an unknown figure. I had subconsciously trapped myself into a world of only making "X" dollars and staying on this wheel of working hard for all that I have.

To help you with this sort of questioning, I like to look at the **Four Questions** from Byron Katie. It can start to give you a chance to look deeper and find out what is true and what is not.

At first glance, these four questions may seem too simple to stir real transformation. But don't be fooled. Simplicity is part of the medicine. When asked with presence and curiosity—from a grounded place inside you—they become a portal. A key. A way to unhook from thoughts you've been dragging around like they're gospel truth.

Let's break this down, one question at a time.

IS IT TRUE?

Pick one sentence from your freewrite that has emotional heat behind it. You'll know it when you see it. It might sound like:

"I'M NOT GOOD ENOUGH."

"NO ONE WANTS WHAT I OFFER."

"IF I SUCCEED, PEOPLE WILL HATE ME."

"I ALWAYS RUIN EVERYTHING."
"IT'S TOO LATE FOR ME TO CHANGE."

Now ask yourself: **Is it true?**

Don't answer automatically. Sit with it. Let the question breathe. Imagine it echoing through the caverns of your nervous system and subconscious. This is where you pause—not to justify or defend the thought, but to really *feel* into whether it holds water. Sometimes the answer will be a soft but firm *yes*. Other times, it will be a surprising *no*. Either way, we're just starting the inquiry. No need to rush.

You can physically feel the answer within your body. If you get that warm fuzzy feeling, often in the heart center, then it is a truth. If it makes you feel sick to your stomach, then it is often false. Heard of the phrase "a gut feeling"? Here you go. This is what they are talking about. The gut is said to have sort of a "brain" for your subconscious, intuitive side. It will tell you when things are right or wrong.

Give it a try. Make a statement that you know is true. Your favorite color works great for this. Say it out loud and then feel it. Where does it land? How does it land? Feels good, right. Now, flip it. Make the statement, "My favorite color is

_____." Fill in the blank with a color you don't like. Now, how does that feel? Gross, right? This is your body responding physically. Playing with this practice is a great way to pave your way to the work we are going to be doing later in this book.

CAN I ABSOLUTELY KNOW THAT IT'S TRUE?

This is where things get juicy. The second question is a scalpel—it cuts through the illusion of certainty.

You may believe, "I'm unlovable," or "I'll never succeed," but can you *absolutely* know that's true? As in 100%, ironclad, cosmic-level truth? Can you know that every person in the world would reject you? That every attempt to succeed is doomed before it starts? That this pain, this pattern, this fear defines *you*?

Spoiler alert: you can't. And that's not to invalidate your experience—it's to loosen the chokehold of belief.

Our thoughts feel like facts when we've rehearsed them a thousand times. But this question invites you to step back and consider that what you *believe* might not be the whole truth. This is where the light starts to crack in.

HOW DO I REACT WHEN I BELIEVE THAT THOUGHT?

This one's important because it invites you to become the observer of your internal experience.

Ask yourself: when you believe that thought, what happens inside you?

HOW DOES YOUR BODY FEEL? TIGHT, NUMB, BRACED?

HOW DO YOU TREAT OTHERS? DO YOU SHRINK, LASH OUT, AVOID?

HOW DO YOU TREAT *YOURSELF*? DO YOU ABANDON, CRITICIZE, SHUT DOWN?

This question isn't meant to shame you. It's here to *show* you how the thought operates in your system. Maybe when you believe "I'm not good enough," you procrastinate. You don't return that email. You isolate. You overeat. You perfectionistically tweak a project into oblivion. You live small.

You start to see that it's not the *truth* of the thought that's driving your behavior—it's your belief in it. And when you're aware of that, you have something you didn't have before: **choice**.

WHO WOULD I BE WITHOUT THAT THOUGHT?

This question turns the whole paradigm on its head. It invites you to imagine, just for a moment, what it would feel like to *not* carry that thought like a badge of identity. Who would you be without the belief that you're unworthy, broken, too much, too late, not enough?

Not "who would you become after years of healing"—but who would you be *right now* without that belief clouding your vision? What would shift in your energy? Your voice? Your posture? Your desire?

Let your imagination run wild here. Maybe you'd be bold. Maybe you'd be soft. Maybe you'd laugh more. Maybe you'd finally exhale. This question reconnects you with the you beneath the programming—the one who's been waiting for permission to just *be*.

PUTTING IT ALL TOGETHER

As you walk yourself through these four questions, keep your journal open. Write down your answers, not to analyze, but to witness what comes through. This is a sacred conversation with your deeper self.

Here are a few pro tips:

DON'T RUSH. GIVE EACH QUESTION TIME TO LAND.

DON'T TRY TO "GET IT RIGHT." LET WHATEVER COMES UP BE
ENOUGH.

DON'T WORRY IF IT FEELS AWKWARD AT FIRST. THAT'S NOR-
MAL. THIS IS UNCHARTED TERRITORY FOR MOST OF US.

And remember: this process isn't about erasing your thoughts. It's about creating space between *you* and the thought. It's about remembering that just because you think it, doesn't mean it's true. And just because you've believed it for years doesn't mean you have to keep carrying it forward.

Your thoughts aren't villains. They're echoes. Of past wounds, old stories, inherited fears. But when you turn toward them with curiosity and love instead of judgment, something starts to shift. You start to reclaim your authority. You stop living on autopilot.

This is where the real reprogramming begins. So take your time. Feel your way through. And know that every belief you dismantle is a step toward freedom.

The Glass Ceiling

By now, you've started to catch glimpses of the patterns that run the show. You see how your stories shape your choices, how autopilot sneaks in under the radar. But there's another layer most people don't see until they hit it headfirst: **the glass ceiling.**

I already mentioned this in the previous chapters but now it's time to really sink our teeth into this concept. This isn't the corporate glass ceiling that continues to keep women from corner offices with vast views of the city around. It's the *internal* one that keeps you from living the life you keep saying you want.

This glass ceiling is built by your nervous system, brick by brick, through years of programming. It whispers: *This much joy is safe. This much success is tolerable. This much love won't kill us.* And the second you start edging beyond it, that alarm goes off once again. Your heart races. Doubt creeps in. You sabotage, stall, or suddenly feel bone-tired. Not because you don't want it badly enough. But because your body equates "more" with "danger."

As mentioned before, Gay Hendricks calls this the **Upper Limit Problem**—the hidden thermostat of how much good you'll allow before you unconsciously turn the heat back down. Jennie Potter calls it your **set points**—the subconscious boundary programmed long before you were old enough to question it. I call it the glass ceiling. And once you find it, you can't lose track of it.

Think about it: your nervous system doesn't give a damn about your dream board or affirmations. Its job is survival. Not thriving, not expansion—just *keep you alive.* And if joy, intimacy, abundance, or peace feel unfamiliar, your system will flag them as unsafe. That means the very things you've been begging for—the healthy love, the financial freedom, the creative breakthrough—can trigger the same alarms as a threat.

That's why you see people win big only to sabotage the hell out of it.

THEY LAND THE DREAM PARTNER... AND PICK FIGHTS.
THEY FINALLY SAVE SOME MONEY... AND BLOW IT ON IMPULSE.

THEY QUIT THE SOUL-SUCKING JOB... AND FIND THEMSELVES RECREATING THE SAME TOXIC DYNAMICS SOMEWHERE ELSE.

It's not laziness. It's not self-hatred. It's the glass ceiling at work. And sure, this does sound a whole lot like our sabotaging behaviors being triggered. However, here's the sickest part: the ceiling doesn't look like sabotage at first. It looks like "being realistic." It shows up as procrastination, "forgetting," or playing small in rooms where you could roar. It feels *rational* to stay under it. That's how it traps you. It doesn't have to show its face through our actions and limited beliefs.

Think about that number on the scale that you just can't seem to pass. You have been working for the past 6 months to lose those final 15 pounds but no matter the workouts you do or the meals you pass on or any of the numerous other self-help practices for weight loss you grind at, you never see that magic number on the scale below your feet. Your body is holding on to a glass ceiling about your weight that feels safe.

Remember though, the ceiling isn't real. It's glass. Transparent. Fragile. The only power it has is the story you've been living under it. So what do you do? You move it.

Sorry but no, that doesn't happen by chanting mantras and hoping your cells fall in line. Moving the ceiling starts with awareness. You have to catch it in the act—when you're about to shrink after a win, when you're scanning for flaws in something good, when you feel the urge to pull back from what you've been asking for. That moment? That's the edge of the glass.

Want the gritty truth? Moving the ceiling doesn't mean it disappears forever. You'll meet it again at the next level. Every time you expand, your system will test you: *Is this safe? Can we hold this?* That's not failure. That's proof you're growing.

I want you to remember something: ceilings are meant to be broken. Glass doesn't shatter quietly. It cracks, splinters, and makes a mess. Sometimes moving the ceiling feels exhilarating. Sometimes it feels terrifying. Sometimes it feels like you're walking barefoot across shards. But what's on the other side? Breathing room. Expansion. Sky.

So the next time you notice yourself shrinking after a win, or itching for sabotage when things finally get good, don't shame yourself. Don't label it as proof you're broken. Smile a little. Because you just found your ceiling. And if you can see it, you can move it.

This is the part most people miss about "success." They think the hard work is getting the thing—landing the partner, the raise, the breakthrough. But the real work is *holding it without collapse.* Living beyond the ceiling without scrambling back to the familiar ground of "just enough."

That's the work of integration. That's why embodiment matters. That's why nervous system safety is non-negotiable. Because until your body trusts more, your ceiling stays put.

So let me ask you: what would it feel like to not just break the ceiling—but raise it? To keep nudging it higher every time you expand, until one day you look up and realize there's no ceiling left—just open sky?

That's not fantasy. That's the trajectory when you choose to stop mistaking safety for freedom. And that's the truth your old operating system never wanted you to know: the ceiling was never locked. The only thing keeping it in place was you forgetting that you could move it. You'll meet this ceiling again when we hit integration. For now, just notice it.

Every ceiling you hit is stitched together by shadow. The moments you were taught that love equals loss, that success equals punishment, that joy equals danger. When you meet the ceiling, you're really meeting your shadow. And that's where truth-telling turns into shadow integration—the work of facing the protector parts and inviting them into a new story.

The Pursuit of the Shadow

So you've spilled the ink. You've uncovered the thoughts. You've held them up to the light and questioned their truth. But here's the thing—just because you've explored the thoughts doesn't mean you've yet met the shadow behind them.

This is where the real pursuit begins.

Carl Jung, the godfather of shadow work, reminds us:

ONE DOES NOT BECOME ENLIGHTENED BY
IMAGINING FIGURES OF LIGHT, BUT BY MAKING
THE DARKNESS CONSCIOUS.

In other words, growth doesn't happen by skipping straight to the positive. It happens when you bravely turn toward what you've buried. You don't heal by pretending the pain isn't there—you heal by seeing it clearly, naming it, and integrating it back into wholeness.

Now, it's time to go back into your writing—but not with a pen. With a flashlight. Read through your freewrite and the takeaways like a detective scanning a case file. What's the emotional residue left behind in the words? Is it shame? Rage? Guilt? Resentment? Fear? Longing?

Your shadow isn't just one thing—it's a collection of unconscious identities built to protect you. And they often don't speak in absolutes. They show up in the subtle patterns. In phrases like:

"I can't trust anyone."
"I always mess things up."
"If I succeed, I'll be alone."
"If I ask for more, I'll lose everything."

Beneath those lines are identities. Archetypes. Personas you've crafted for survival. This is the part of the process where you begin to name the shadow—not to shame it, but to recognize it. To say, "Ah. There you are."

This is where we connect back to Chapter 3. Remember all those saboteur archetypes we explored? The Overachiever. The People-Pleaser. The Rebel. The Martyr. The Victim. The Critic. The Chameleon. The Lone Wolf. These weren't just clever names—they were roadmaps. Emotional blueprints for how your unconscious has tried to keep you safe by keeping you small.

Now's the time to revisit that gallery of archetypes and see which ones show up in your writing. Are you seeing the fingerprints of the Addict who numbs instead of feeling? The Gatekeeper who doesn't let success in? The Romanticizer who clings to fantasy over truth? For a full list of the archetypes and some key points to each of them, find the reference guide in the back of the book.

There's no wrong answer here. Sometimes, multiple shadows will appear in one free write. That's okay. Let them all pull up a chair.

In my own takeaways shared above, I found that I have The Victim and The Martyr playing out in my resistance to financial abundance. I would blame others for my lack and then in the same breath want to stand up on my soapbox and start a riot to take down "the man". Fueling others to take part in my personal injustices from the 1%. I was literally keeping myself stuck financially by spitting words of disgust to the very person I would wish to become. Mind fucking blown!

This step is deeply Jungian—shadow work is not about exorcising these parts of you, but embracing them with compassion. As Jung said, **"Until you make the unconscious conscious, it will direct your life and you will call it fate."**

This is your moment of direction. Of naming. Of reclaiming power from the parts of you that have been silently pulling the strings. When you give the shadow a name, it loses its grip. Because what is owned can no longer control you.

So revisit your words. Cross-reference them with the archetypes. Look for tone, pattern, and pain. You'll know when it lands because you'll feel it in your gut. That moment of "Oof. That's me."

And when you feel it?

Say hello. Don't resist. Welcome it in. Because the truth is: the parts of you that you hide are often the parts with the most power.

The Shadow in the Wild: A Week of Radical Observation

Okay, you've named the shadow and saboteur. You've written it out, raw and uncensored. You've questioned the thoughts it's built on using Byron Katie's four-question excavation. Now what?

Now, we watch. Like the lioness hunting her prey or those "bird watchers" from their living room windows, binoculars in hand, notepad in lap. I know what you are really do-ing...gathering juicy gossip for your bridge club gals. Sor-ry...okay back to us. Now, we watch.

Not with judgment. Not with the urgency to fix or cleanse or solve. But with the eyes of a curious, grounded witness. You are about to spend a week doing what most people never do: consciously observing the shadow and sabotage patterns that have been steering the wheel of your life from the backseat.

Why does this matter?

Because when you observe without interference, you give the subconscious enough room to speak clearly. You see your own habits not as character flaws or failures, but as brilliant adaptations. You start to track the map of how this pattern lives and breathes inside your system. And in that witnessing? Power. Precision. Choice.

This is shadow work in the wild. Let's break it down.

STEP ONE: BECOME THE ANTHROPOLOGIST OF YOUR OWN LIFE

You are not going into this next week as a judge. You're going in as an anthropologist—a neutral observer of your internal terrain. Your job isn't to change anything. Your job is to **watch** how this specific shadow or sabotage pattern shows up in real time.

Do you procrastinate right after receiving good news?

Do you over-prepare before a simple task because you're afraid of being seen as incompetent?

Do you people-please when you actually want to scream?

Do you numb out with food, scrolling, perfectionism, or planning?

Note it. Name it. Don't try to change it yet. Just track it. And more importantly—**feel it**.

Notice what happens in your body when the pattern activates. Does your throat tighten? Your stomach sink? Your jaw clench? Where does the energy go? What emotion is present? This is somatic intelligence, and it's crucial for the rewiring process later. But first, we track it.

Step Two: Identify the Triggers

Every shadow pattern has a set of conditions that bring it to life. These are your triggers. They can be external (like a bossy email or a tense conversation) or internal (like the fear of success, a wave of shame, or even boredom).

Throughout your day, pause and ask:

WHAT JUST HAPPENED?
WHAT DID I FEEL RIGHT BEFORE THIS REACTION?
WHAT THOUGHTS POPPED UP IN MY MIND?
WHAT BELIEF DID THIS MOMENT CONFIRM OR CHALLENGE?

This isn't about spiraling into over-analysis. It's about gentle awareness. You're teaching yourself to **see the invisible leash** that's been tugging you around.

Example:

You set aside time to work on your creative project, but suddenly feel exhausted and start scrolling instead. Pause. What triggered that shift? Was it the blank page? The fear of failure? The thought that your idea isn't original?

Note it. That's a breadcrumb.

STEP THREE: MAP THE LOOP

By the end of a few days, you'll start seeing the same pattern loop on repeat. It might have different costumes—today it looks like perfectionism, yesterday it looked like avoidance—but it's the same core shadow playing dress-up.

Map the cycle. It might look something like this:

INSPIRATION HITS → YOU FEEL EXCITED
YOU TAKE ACTION → DOUBT CREEPS IN
SHADOW ACTIVATES → "WHAT IF I FAIL?"
BODY REACTS → TIGHT CHEST, SHALLOW BREATH
SELF-SOOTHING RESPONSE → NETFLIX, SNACKS, PERFEC-
TIONIST PLANNING

SHAME HANGOVER → "WHY CAN'T I FOLLOW THROUGH?"
RESET INTENTION → TRY AGAIN TOMORROW

This map is gold. It's your sabotage ritual in action. And once you know the steps, you can start disrupting them—*but not yet.* First, you just need to see it. Fully. Clearly. Without shame.

STEP FOUR: GET PLAYFULLY HONEST

Want to make this even more powerful? Narrate your sabotage moments like a wildlife documentary.

"This morning, Erin sat down to complete her big project. But alas, the shadow emerged, subtle and sly. Watch closely as she suddenly remembers she needs to reorganize the spice rack. Ah yes, a classic redirection technique used by the Saboteur when faced with vulnerability."

This isn't just silly—it's effective. Humor helps disarm shame. And the less shame you have around your patterns, the more capacity you have to change them. Plus, it primes us for later steps as we integrate the shadow into the light.

So play. Laugh. Narrate. And let it be weird.

STEP FIVE: LOG THE HIGHLIGHTS

Each night, jot down what you noticed that day. Not a five-page journal entry—just a quick list or voice memo:

SHADOW SHOWED UP WHEN I FELT IGNORED IN A MEETING.
I WANTED TO SAY NO, BUT SAID YES OUT OF GUILT.
BODY RESPONSE: HEAVY CHEST, FLUSHED FACE.

OLD BELIEF: "IF I SPEAK UP, I'LL BE REJECTED."

You are collecting data, not proving a theory. The goal isn't to fix—it's to witness with clarity and compassion.

WHAT THIS PRACTICE CREATES

Spending a full week in observation mode slows down your inner world long enough for you to catch the patterns in real time. It builds your self-awareness muscles. It quiets the internal chaos. And perhaps most importantly—it begins to loosen the shame grip.

Because when you stop seeing your patterns as proof that you're broken, and start seeing them as adaptive survival strategies? You reclaim your power. You step out of judgment and into authority.

You don't have to make any massive changes during this week. You just have to notice. Because once you've seen your shadow's dance in the wild, you'll never again believe it's just who you are.

You'll know it's a pattern. And patterns can be changed.

But first... they must be seen.

Five

WHERE IT LIVES

Somatic Shadow Integration

W e've danced with the shadow on paper. We've questioned our looping thoughts. We've watched our sabotage slither through our daily life like a well-rehearsed magician's trick—predictable, slippery, and just barely out of reach. And now? Now we drop deeper.

Into the body.

Because the truth is, your shadow doesn't just live in your mind. It's not some philosophical concept floating in the ethers of your intellect. It's *in you*. Burrowed into your muscles. Tucked behind your diaphragm. Coiled in your pelvis. Whispering in the back of your throat when you go to speak your truth. Your shadow is a somatic experience—a living, breathing imprint on your nervous system.

You can journal it. You can analyze it. You can even give it a name and a whole archetype gallery like we did in Chapter 3. But until you *feel* where it lives, until you drop into the rawness of its residence, you're just doing mental gymnastics around the wound.

This chapter is where we stop circling and start sinking. This is the work that goes below the neck. Because insight alone doesn't shift patterns—*embodiment does*.

Welcome to the sacred process of somatic shadow integration. This isn't about fixing yourself. This isn't a spiritual exorcism or a mental detox. This is about meeting the exact place in your body where the sabotage has been trying to keep you safe. Where it has taken up residence like a loyal but misunderstood guardian.

And here's what might surprise you—it doesn't feel "bad." Not always. Sometimes it shows up as a heaviness in your chest, or a clenching in your gut. Sometimes it's a sense of buzzing in your hands, a tightness in your throat, a sudden urge to flee or freeze. Your body holds the score, as the saying goes. And in this chapter, we're finally going to read it.

We will use a modified process inspired by the Existential Kink method—because, yes, it *is* possible to love the part of you that self-sabotages. To not just understand it, but to give it gratitude. That's how true integration happens. Not by slaying the shadow, but by acknowledging the brilliance of how it once tried to protect you. To fit you into your childhood environment. To help you survive.

So as we begin, I ask you to slow down. Breathe. And get ready to meet the physical imprint of your subconscious patterns. This is the foundation for everything that comes next—clearing, transmuting, manifesting. But before we can release what no longer serves us, we have to know where it lives.

And now, we're going in.

Why the Body?

Cognitive insight can get us far. But it doesn't complete the shift. You can understand your pattern, label your archetype, and mentally "get it"—but if your body still braces in fear every time you're seen, no amount of insight will move the needle. As trauma expert Bessel van der Kolk said, *"The body keeps the score."* And it's in the body where the transformation really sticks.

Energetically, emotionally, biologically—your body is storing information from your past. It remembers the betrayals, the abandonment, the fear of not being enough. It also remembers the moments when shrinking, numbing, or lashing out worked. The shadow patterns didn't arise out of nowhere. They were adaptive strategies. And your body? It never forgets.

This is where we move from analysis to alchemy. Because the body doesn't lie. You might rationalize a pattern in your mind, but your stomach still knots when you speak up. Your chest still tightens when money's low. Your jaw still clenches when you set a boundary. These reactions are *somatic imprints*—embedded not just in your thoughts, but in your tissue, your nervous system, your energy field.

Carolyn Elliott, in *Existential Kink*, talks about the paradoxical pleasure we derive from these patterns. That some part of us—the unconscious part—actually *enjoys* the sabotage, because it confirms what we already believe to be true.

"SEE? I REALLY AM TOO MUCH."
"I KNEW I'D SCREW IT UP."
"THEY ALWAYS LEAVE."

That confirmation brings a strange comfort. A twisted sense of control. Because if we can predict the pain, at least we aren't blindsided by it. At least we are the ones pulling the strings.

This is what Elliott calls *kinky*. Not in the sexual sense (though sometimes that too), but in the way our psyche gets off on staying stuck. There's a pleasure in the familiarity. A satisfaction in being right—even if "right" means miserable. It's why we replay certain emotional loops over and over, not because we like the suffering, but because the suffering is *known*. Predictable. Safe in a very unsafe-feeling world.

The shadow doesn't just hide pain—it hides *power*. It's where your unmet needs, disowned desires, and suppressed instincts live. And your body? It's the first place that power gets stored, distorted, and locked away. That's why we go into the body—not to fix it, but to feel it. To reclaim what we've hidden, even from ourselves.

This chapter isn't about exorcising your shadow. It's about integrating it. It's about reclaiming the parts of you that were cast out, instead of casting them out again. Meeting your shadow in the body. Honoring what it's done for you—even as you gently ask it to release its grip. Because your body isn't just a vessel for the past, but also the portal for your liberation.

John Ruskan, in *Emotional Clearing*, insists that true healing doesn't come from intellectual insight alone—it comes from *presence*. Not the performative kind of presence we sometimes fake in mindfulness memes, but the gritty, embodied kind. The kind where you feel the tightness in your chest, the twisting in your gut, the heat behind your eyes—and instead of moving away from it, you stay. You feel it. You let it be exactly as it is.

Ruskan's method isn't about manipulating the emotion or trying to coax it into being more manageable. He's not asking you to analyze where the emotion came from or to trace it back to a specific trauma (although those insights may arise naturally). What he teaches is deceptively simple and profoundly difficult: allow the emotion to be felt in the body without resistance. Don't judge it. Don't force it to change. Just *feel it all the way through*.

This act of pure witnessing is what he calls *emotional clearing*—not because you're pushing anything out, but because the emotion, when met with full, nonjudgmental awareness, begins to resolve on its own. It completes its cycle. The energy that was frozen or distorted in your system starts to move again, like a thaw after a long winter.

And where does this witnessing happen? Not in your thoughts. Not in your story. It happens in the body.

The body is where the charge lives. The body is where the sabotage pattern took root. That lump in your throat? That rock in your belly? That buzzing in your jaw? That *is* the shadow, wrapped in sensation. Locating that sensation is the first portal into integration. Because once you feel it without trying to change it, you start to reclaim the power that was being held hostage.

This is not about wallowing in the emotion or drowning in it. It's about *being with it long enough to transmute it*. As Ruskan reminds us, healing happens when we stop interfering with our internal experience and start relating to the emotion directly, with honesty and neutrality. When we let the body guide the process, we stop trying to "solve" our sabotage and instead *dissolve* it—through feeling, not force.

Let's get even more granular: Your nervous system—especially your autonomic nervous system—is wired for survival and doesn't care about your goals or your insight. It only cares about keeping you safe. Safety is determined by *felt* sense, not logic. So if being seen previously led to rejection, or standing up for yourself at one time triggered punishment, your body learns: "This is unsafe. We won't do this again."

From that point forward, even years later, your system will respond accordingly. You may feel nauseous before speaking. Your chest might tighten when someone compliments you. You might procrastinate or pick a fight when you get close to a breakthrough. And you'll wonder why you can't "just do the thing"—but your body isn't being difficult. It's doing *exactly* what it was programmed to do: protect.

This is why we must include the body in shadow work. Not just as a source of intuition, but as a vital participant in the healing process. This is why, when we locate where the pattern lives in the body, we're not just identifying tension—we're finding the portal. The access point to real integration.

Because you cannot integrate what you won't feel. And you cannot feel what you won't find.

So yes, we need the stories. The archetypes. The insight. But now, we're moving from theory into practice. From ideas into embodiment. From asking "Why do I do this?" to asking "Where does this live in me now?"

As you move into the next section, I'll walk you through a process I call the **Somatic Integration Method**—a synthesis inspired by *Existential Kink*, grounded in the emotional presence of *Emotional Clearing*, and held in the radical compassion of Jungian integration. You're going to find the place in your body where the sabotage still hums. You're going to feel it—fully. And then, instead of banishing it, you're going to do something revolutionary.

You're going to thank it.

Because your shadow wasn't born to ruin you. It was born to *protect* you. And now that you're older, wiser, and stronger, you get to let it off duty—with gratitude, not guilt.

Let's begin.

Welcome to the Somatic Integration Method (SI Method)

This is the process you'll return to again and again throughout this part of the journey. It's designed to help you locate the emotional pattern in your body, acknowledge the protective role it's played, and integrate the shadow—not through analysis, but through presence, sensation, and gratitude.

STEP ONE: LOCATE THE PATTERN

Think back to the block or goal you've been working with. Bring it gently into your awareness—not the original wound, not the deepest trauma, but a **recent trigger** that feels emotionally charged. Something that reflects the pattern you're ready to shift. Maybe it was that job opportunity you talked yourself out of. The argument that left you spiraling. The time you felt like the outsider in the high school cafeteria. The moment you almost posted your offer but froze. Let it come forward—not to relive it, but to observe it.

Now, ask yourself: **Where do I feel this in my body?**

Close your eyes. Not now, obviously. I want you to keep reading. Do this later after you finish this chapter. Okay, back to the instructions. Slow everything down. Begin a body scan—not with judgment, but with curiosity. Start at the crown of your head. Gently move your awareness down through your face, jaw, neck... your shoulders, arms, hands... chest, ribs, solar plexus, belly... pelvis, hips, thighs... knees, calves, ankles, and feet.

Where does your attention catch or linger? Where does something feel... different? Dense? Tight? Charged? Maybe there's heat. Maybe it's numbness. Maybe it pulses or stings or hums. You're not looking for something dramatic—you're looking for what's **alive**. Subtle counts. Stillness counts. Even that absence of feeling might be the signal.

This is where the shadow is showing itself—**not as a thought, but as sensation.**

Describe it clearly in your journal:

WHAT IS THE SENSATION?

DOES IT HAVE A SHAPE OR TEXTURE? A TEMPERATURE?

IF IT HAD A COLOR, WHAT WOULD IT BE?

IS IT MOVING OR STILL? EXPANDING OR CONTRACTING?

DOES IT FEEL FAMILIAR? FOREIGN?

For example:

"IT FEELS LIKE A HOT COIL IN THE CENTER OF MY CHEST, RED AND THROBBING."

"THERE'S A DULL ACHE BEHIND MY EYES, LIKE FOG."

"A TIGHT BALL IN MY SOLAR PLEXUS THAT FEELS LIKE CLENCHED FISTS."

This somatic pinpointing is not optional—it's essential. It's what turns the abstract concept of "sabotage" into something tangible. Real. Locatable. And once you can feel it, you can begin to **work with it**. You're no longer just analyzing the pattern—you're engaging with its physical imprint. This is where the shift begins.

For me, I had traced this heavy mucky feeling along the right side of my neck and across my collarbone when I was looking into my procrastination and perfectionism. I was working on my marketing blocks and why I couldn't seem to get myself started with producing videos for my idea of a YouTube channel. The feeling was almost this sinking feeling.

I want to take a moment to point out that even though you are feeling this pain in one area of your body for this specific trigger, you will feel it in another location when looking at another goal or shift you want to make. For example, even though I was feeling the heavy sinking feeling in my neck and collarbones when thinking about the procrastination and perfectionism of my marketing woes, the sensation will be different when I think of the procrastination or perfectionism of another area in my life, let's say with relationships. Or maybe with even writing a book...ahem.

Clearing one area doesn't automatically clear them all. It doesn't work like that. This is a process. You have been collecting these sabotaging behaviors your entire life, so clearing it once in only a few minutes doesn't release the pattern completely from your life.

STEP TWO: FEEL IT FULLY

Now that you've located the sensation—where the pattern physically lives in your body—your only job is to stay with it. Don't analyze. Don't problem-solve. Don't try to get rid of it. Just feel it. Let the story take a backseat for now. You're not thinking your way out of the sabotage—you're feeling your way through it.

This is the *felt sense*, a term used by somatic psychologist Eugene Gendlin. It's not just the presence of emotion; it's the physical awareness of emotion before it fully takes shape in the mind. It's raw, unfiltered. And it speaks in sensation.

Let yourself drop in.

Breathe into it gently. No need to force a big emotional release. Simply *be* with the texture of the sensation—tightness, buzzing, heat, numbness, whatever it is. Notice what emotion begins to rise. Is there sadness? Guilt? Fury? Fear? Sometimes it's a cocktail of all of them. That's okay.

Whatever comes up, let it unfold. No judgment. No editing. You're not here to remove it in this moment—you're here to witness it.

As you stay present, the energy might begin to shift or move. You may notice it traveling—often downward. This is common. These deeper emotional frequencies tend to migrate toward the core of the body: the belly, the pelvis, the root. These are primal zones. Places where the nervous system stores its oldest memories and where the subconscious often tucks away its most potent protections.

This is the territory Jung referred to as the *shadow unconscious*—the hidden reservoir of our disowned instincts, wounds, and potential. And this is why you're here. You're not chasing a feeling; you're allowing the feeling to reveal something to you.

The moment you stop resisting what you feel, the moment you choose to witness rather than suppress—you begin the alchemy. You tell your body, "You don't have to hold this alone anymore."

This is how integration begins—not with insight, but with presence.

Step Three: Recognize the Protector

This is where the deeper wisdom of *Existential Kink* truly begins to shine through.

The sensation you're feeling—this heaviness in the chest, this clench in the jaw, this ache in the belly—isn't just discomfort. It's not just pain. It's protection. It's a signal from a part of you that once had a job: to keep you safe.

This part of you—this reaction, this pattern, this inner protector—was born out of necessity. Not malice. Not weakness. It arose in response to something that once felt too overwhelming, too dangerous, or too unknown to process at the time.

Maybe it's the freeze response that helped you survive a volatile parent. Maybe it's the contraction in your throat that helped you stay silent when speaking up would have gotten you punished. Maybe it's the apathy or dissociation that helped you numb out when your heart broke and no one came to comfort you.

These responses weren't failures. They were strategies. They were brilliant. They were adaptive. And they worked—until now.

Existential Kink teaches us that these patterns often carry with them a hidden kink: a strange, paradoxical pleasure in the familiar discomfort. Because if we know how the pain plays out, we stay in control. If we expect disappointment, we never risk the crash of surprise. That clenching feeling? It's not just fear—it's mastery. "See? I knew they'd leave." "I was right to hold back." "Good thing I didn't hope too hard."

Now it's time to thank the part that played this role.

Say to it:

"I see you. I know you were trying to help me. Thank you."

Let it land. Don't rush it. You may even want to place a hand on that part of your body. Breathe into it. Let your gratitude be real.

This is the turning point in the Somatic Integration (SI) Method. You're not here to fight your shadow. You're not here to shame it. You're here to recognize it for what it really is—a younger, instinctive part of you that did its best. And when that part is seen, acknowledged, and appreciated, its grip begins to soften.

John Ruskan, in *Emotional Clearing*, reinforces this with his teachings in Chapters 11 and 13: Feel the emotion fully, without judgment, and it begins to process itself. The block isn't the problem. Resisting the block is.

This is a turning point—not just emotionally, but energetically.

When you recognize the shadow not as a saboteur to silence, but as a protector to honor, something begins to shift. The emotional charge softens. The contraction loosens. You begin to reclaim a piece of your power that's been tied up in fear or shame. And even if you don't feel instantly "better," your frequency begins to change.

That's not just a nice idea—it's physics. Every emotion has a vibration. And when you meet an old frequency with presence, compassion, and gratitude, you start to transmute it. Slowly. Gently. Cell by cell. Breath by breath.

We'll come back to this shift soon—because it's the foundation for everything that follows. The vibrational change you're starting to feel here? That's the seed we'll water when we begin stepping into manifestation.

But for now, stay in the presence. Stay in the gratitude. You don't have to rush the light.

STEP FOUR: HONOR AND SURRENDER

As you stay with the feeling—holding it with presence and compassion instead of fear—something begins to shift. Slowly, the tightness may begin to loosen. The charge may start to dissolve. This isn't forced. It isn't logical. It's energetic and deeply felt. You're no longer fighting the shadow. You're seeing it, honoring it, and offering it a seat at the table.

This is where we surrender—not by giving up, but by giving over the struggle. We stop bracing against the pattern and start bowing to the intelligence that created it.

Say to this part of you:

"THANK YOU FOR PROTECTING ME."
"THANK YOU FOR KEEPING ME SAFE WHEN I DIDN'T KNOW HOW."
"THANK YOU FOR BEING HERE ALL THIS TIME."

And then, say this:

"I DON'T NEED YOU TO WORK SO HARD ANYMORE."
"YOU'VE DONE ENOUGH. YOU CAN REST NOW."

Let the words be a vibration, not just a thought. Let them ripple through your chest, your belly, your bones. Imagine this energy—this shadow, this protector—as a tired soldier returning from battle. You're not banishing it. You're welcoming it home. You're releasing it from duty.

This is where integration truly happens—not in fighting the pattern, but in loving it.

You might notice physical signs of this surrender. A softening in the shoulders. A spontaneous sigh. A wave of heat or even tears. These aren't signs of breakdown. They're signs of letting go. Signs that your nervous system is receiving the message: *It's okay now. We're safe.* In the words of Martha Stewart, "It's a good thing."

This is the art of somatic shadow integration—not a dramatic exorcism, but a quiet reunion. You're reclaiming energy that's been locked away in fear and shame and letting it return to you as wisdom and power. And this shift? This emotional recalibration? It matters.

In later chapters, we'll come back to this moment—this vibrational shift—and explore how it creates the foundation for aligned action, higher emotional frequencies, and even quantum manifestation. But for now, let this be enough.

Let the honoring be the healing. Let the surrender be the liberation. Let your body remember what it feels like to say: *You don't have to protect me anymore. I've got this now.*

A Note on Safety

Important: Before you go any deeper into this work, here's something I want you to hold close:

This is not a trauma excavation mission.

You are not required—or even encouraged—to go digging for your deepest, darkest memory to prove you're "doing the work." That's not healing. That's reactivation. And while it might feel dramatic or intense, it doesn't always lead to integration.

We're not here to relive the earthquake. We're here to listen to the aftershocks.

Instead of starting with a core wound or past trauma, begin with something current. Something recent. A stuck loop in your life, a recurring emotion, a difficult interaction, a resistance that keeps coming up. These daily experiences hold echoes of the deeper pattern—and often, they'll lead you exactly where you need to go.

Why do it this way?

Because the body doesn't distinguish between a memory and a moment. If you dive straight into a traumatic root without proper support, your nervous system can go into fight, flight, freeze, or fawn—effectively shutting down your access to presence and awareness, which is the whole point of this practice. That's not integration. That's re-traumatization.

By working with a smaller, present-day trigger—something that still holds charge but isn't overwhelming—you're giving your system the chance to stay *with* the process, not bolt from it. You're learning how to build capacity. How to stay in relationship with your discomfort without being consumed by it.

This approach honors your timing, your safety, and your inner wisdom. It says: *You don't have to go back to the fire to prove you were burned. You can sit with the scar and still do the work.*

So if you start to feel overwhelmed, shut down, or dissociated—pause. Place your hand on your chest or belly. Breathe. Drink water. Look around the room and anchor into the present. You are not back there. You are here. You are safe. And you get to choose how deep you go.

Healing is not a performance. It's a relationship—with your shadow, your nervous system, and your own body's pace. There's no rush. No gold medal for fastest descent into the abyss. There is only truth, readiness, and self-honoring.

You're doing this beautifully. And you're doing it safely. That matters more than anything else.

Integration Isn't Erasure

Let's get one thing straight: you're not trying to *delete* the shadow.

You're not erasing, defeating, or exiling it to some locked vault labeled "healed." That's not how this works. Shadow integration isn't about vanishing the parts of you that once misfired—it's about transforming the relationship you have with them.

As Carl Jung wrote, *"The shadow is a tight passage, a narrow door, whose painful constriction no one is spared who goes down to the deep well."*

You've just walked through that door.

And on the other side? Not purity. Not perfection. But wholeness.

The truth is, the shadow never completely disappears. It gets quieter. Softer. It takes on new forms. Sometimes it even becomes an ally—a signal that you're nearing the edge of expansion. A sacred discomfort that shows up when you're about to break a pattern. Not to sabotage, but to say, "We're entering new terrain. Are we safe? Are we ready?"

Your job isn't to eliminate it. Your job is to recognize it *faster*. To listen without fear. To lovingly re-center when it flares up. That's integration.

You may still feel tension in your belly before you speak up. You may still hesitate before raising your rates or leaving the relationship. But now, you know *why*. You've located the pulse. You've felt the root. You've looked it in the eye. And that awareness alone changes everything.

Because you're not reacting blindly anymore. You're responding with choice. With compassion. With presence.

That's what makes this work so potent. It's not some dramatic overnight awakening. It's subtle. Embodied. It builds like a frequency shift—quiet at first, but impossible to ignore once you've tuned in.

So before we move into the energetic work of Chapter 6—before we talk about clearing and pulling blocks and rewriting patterns—pause here.

Breathe.

Feel the space you've just opened inside you. That space is not emptiness. It's possibility. It's power. It's the void from which something new can emerge.

You've met the body of your sabotage. You didn't run. You didn't fix. You stayed.

You thanked it. You surrendered its grip. And in doing so, you reclaimed something far more valuable than any quick fix could offer.

This... *is the shift.*

Six

CLearing the Saboteur

Energy, Intention, and the Art of Letting Go

B y now, you've met the body of your sabotage. You've felt its presence, located it with precision, and allowed yourself to witness its emotion without resistance. That alone is a kind of medicine—one that most people spend their entire lives avoiding. But the work doesn't stop there. If anything, this is where the deepest layer begins.

This next phase of your journey is where things might start to feel... different. Less analytical. More subtle. Here, we move into the terrain of energetic clearing. And for some, that word—*energy*—can trigger resistance. It can conjure images of vague spiritual practices or new-age detachment. But energy, in the context of healing, is not esoteric. It is experiential. It is lived. It is what you've already been doing every time your chest tightens with anxiety or your stomach knots at the thought of rejection. That's energy in motion—energy trying to get your attention.

Bruce Lipton, in *The Biology of Belief*, reminds us that every cell in the body responds not only to chemical messages, but to the energetic signals we emit—consciously or unconsciously. Emotion, in its most basic form, is *energy in motion*. And when that motion is interrupted—when we suppress, resist, or freeze around a certain emotional experience—it doesn't vanish. It settles. It anchors into the soft tissues, the fascia, the nervous system, and the subconscious. It becomes a holding pattern.

This is what Dr. Bradley Nelson describes in *The Emotion Code* as a "trapped emotion"—an energetic charge that remains embedded in the body long after the mind has moved on. These trapped emotions, he argues, can distort the energy field, affect physical health, and perpetuate emotional loops that no longer serve us. And the way we release them isn't by talking about them or reliving the trauma—it's by gently acknowledging the imprint and inviting the body to let it go.

That's what this chapter is about: noticing where the energy has lingered... and clearing the channel so something new can take root.

Jennie Potter, in *Self-Sabotage No More*, also speaks to the importance of energetic awareness when shifting deeply rooted patterns. She reminds us that many of our sabotaging behaviors are not driven by the conscious mind at all. They live in the unconscious and in the body, often showing up as a set point we keep returning to, despite our best intentions. We override this set point not with willpower, but with integration. And integration requires us to work with the very energy that's holding the pattern in place.

Energetic clearing is not about doing more—it's about becoming present with what is. It's not about bypassing emotion—it's about giving it room to move. And it doesn't require you to become a healer or energy worker. You don't need special tools. You don't need anyone else's permission. You have a body. You have awareness. That's enough.

What we're doing in this chapter is simple, but not easy. We are learning how to become attuned to the invisible architecture of emotion in the body. How to clear not just the mental residue of sabotage, but the somatic tension it leaves behind. Because if we don't clear the charge, we stay stuck in the loop. Insight without energetic movement eventually becomes another form of resistance.

It sounds harsh, but it's true. You can understand your patterns all day long. You can name your archetypes, map your childhood, explain your wounds like a scholar. But if that awareness never moves into the body—if it never stirs the energy beneath the story—it hardens. It calcifies. It becomes just another strategy to stay safe, to stay in control, to stay stuck. Insight becomes armor. A clever way to avoid the deeper vulnerability of actually feeling and transforming.

Because here's the truth: your nervous system doesn't speak in insight. It speaks in sensations, in feelings. And until the energy behind the insight has somewhere to go—until it's felt, released, integrated—it stays trapped in the system. You might have a breakthrough in the mind, but the body never gets the memo.

And when that happens, all that awareness starts to loop. You keep learning more, but shifting less.

That's the trap of over-analysis. The spiritual bypass in a prettier outfit. And it's why energetic work matters. Because real change doesn't just land in your thoughts. It ripples into your breath, your muscles, your field. It moves.

And if it doesn't move? It becomes resistance dressed up as progress.

Think of Sheldon Cooper from *The Big Bang Theory*—brilliant, insightful, and utterly disconnected from emotional embodiment. He is full of all of this sweet, sweet knowledge but is unable to connect with humans on an emotional/energetic level. He knows everything *about* quantum physics, but he's unable to move with it. Insight becomes his fortress. His intellect doesn't open the door to transformation—it keeps it locked.

As we continue, remember: knowing is the first step. But feeling is the turning point.

Before we begin, take a moment to pause. Breathe. Feel into what brought you here. Remember that this work is not about becoming someone else. It's about remembering what's already yours, beneath the static and the protection.

Why We Clear

Every thought, belief, and emotion has a frequency. Not in a metaphorical way, but in a literal, measurable sense. Emotion is energy in motion—until it's not. Until it gets stuck. And when that happens, it leaves a residue. A signal. A tension in the body that doesn't seem to go away, no matter how many affirmations you tape to your mirror. Can you hear my eyes rolling? Oy!

You might not even notice it at first. Because that lump in your throat, the ache in your chest, the tension in your jaw—it becomes your normal. You adjust around it. You medicate it with over-the-counter-medications. You write it off as allergies or the weather. That is until you try to reach for something different. Until you stretch toward change. That's when you feel it: the invisible wall. The self-sabotage. The mysterious fatigue. The resistance you can't quite explain.

That's the block, honey. Welcome to the club.

And clearing the block isn't about erasing your experiences or masking your thoughts and emotions. It's about restoring your flow. It's energetic hygiene. Like brushing your emotional teeth or taking a spiritual shower. It's not something you do once—it's something you return to. Again and again. With compassion. With practice. With presence.

We clear not because there's something wrong with us, but because we've been carrying more than we were meant to hold.

Our nervous system is brilliant. It stores everything it can't process in the moment—like stuffing emotions into the closet when company comes over (or the oven and dishwasher...just sayin'). But closets get full. And eventually, things spill out in unexpected ways: chronic stress, repeated patterns, mood swings, fatigue, autoimmune flare-ups, looping thoughts. And when talking about shadows, the repressed shadow will explode in some of the most embarrassing ways and least expected of times. Exposing our ugly.

So when we clear, we're making space for the present. We are not crowding that scared animal in the corner looking for a way out. Clearing our energy blocks gives a way for our bodies to calm and reclaim its true nature.

Energetic clearing works because the body and the energy field are interconnected. The fascia—your body's connective tissue—is filled with receptors that record emotional memory. When we store emotion somatically, it often lodges in the fascia, muscles, and organs. And when that emotion is met with full awareness—without judgment or force—the energy begins to move again. It unfreezes. It flows.

That's what we're doing here. Not forcing. But inviting the body to complete what it never got to finish. That sigh you suddenly let out? That tear you didn't expect? That sensation of heat or tingling or space returning to your chest? That's energy moving. That's the work, working.

This is also where we deepen into the *Somatic Integration Method*. Because locating the pattern is only the beginning. Once we find it and feel it, we honor its intelligence. Then it is time to take hold and rip it out—with love of course. And when it is removed, the system recalibrates.

Clearing is not some mystical ooga-booga trick for people who don't like science. It *is* science. It's neurobiology. It's quantum physics. It's resonance. And it's your body's own language, asking to be heard.

So no, you're not just being dramatic. That stuckness is real. And yes, there's a way through it.

What Are Energetic Blocks?

Let's define the thing most people feel but can't quite name.

Energetic blocks are places in your system—physical, emotional, and energetic—where your life force no longer flows freely. They're not random. They're patterned. Intelligent, even. And they show up in a number of ways:

A TIGHTENING IN THE THROAT THAT RETURNS EVERY TIME YOU TRY TO SPEAK UP

A FOGGINESS IN YOUR HEAD WHEN IT'S TIME TO MAKE A BIG DECISION

A WEIGHT IN YOUR CHEST THAT NO AMOUNT OF DEEP BREATHING SEEMS TO LIFT

CHRONIC TENSION IN YOUR JAW, BELLY, OR LOWER BACK

EMOTIONS THAT FEEL STUCK ON LOOP, NO MATTER HOW MUCH YOU PROCESS THEM

These aren't just quirks or bad habits. They're messages. Somatic signals from a system that once needed protection—and now needs permission to let go.

In many healing modalities, these are referred to as trapped emotions or energy disturbances. Some practitioners describe them as energetic knots, balls of compressed emotion, or even frequency distortions. While language may vary, the underlying concept remains the same: these blocks are frozen echoes of unprocessed experience.

They form when something big happens—grief, anger, fear, shame—and we don't have the tools, support, or capacity to fully feel it. So instead of flowing through, the emotion settles in. The body, being the loyal protector it is, says, "Don't worry. I'll hold this for you." And hold it, it does.

I think back to all of the times I have heard or even said, "Suck it up." "Just keep swimming. Just keep swimming." "Don't show them your pain and let them win." Our culture literally tells us not to move the energy through. Not because it was being sadistic but because we forgot to add: "Suck it up and let it out." "Shake it off." "Dust yourself off and hop back on the saddle." "Hold space for your pain and honor it but then show them how you are able to grow from it and evolve beyond them." We need to do both the mental work and the somatic work. Okay, back to energy blocks...

Some schools of thought visualize these blocks as literal energy clusters the size of baseballs—or even grapefruits—lodged in the energetic field or embedded in muscle tissue. This is how I often find energy blocks within my clients. However, I have felt worm or spaghetti like energy blocks, cloudy forms of cotton candy fogging up the system, and sharp ice berg like structures hidden away in the energy fields. Whether or not you resonate with that level of imagery doesn't matter. What matters is that you've *felt* it. You've lived with it. You've bumped up against it every time you tried to rise and felt something inside you pull back.

Have you ever taken a big breath in and forced the air from your body only to find it trips or catches a bit in the body? That is what I call an energy block. Try it now. Take a deep inhale. Fill your whole body up with air. Now, push the air from your body fast as if someone just gut punched you. Did you have a catch in the body somewhere? Even taking several of these deep clearing breaths can loosen and even move the stagnant energy from the body.

What we're doing now isn't about proving anything. It's about *tuning in*. Because whether you're visual or not, your body knows where the disruption is. It knows what parts are frozen, inflamed, bracing for impact.

In this work, we don't approach the body like a battlefield. We don't fight the blocks—we *listen* to them. We get curious. We feel the vibration of the emotion beneath the resistance. And that alone begins the release.

Yes, other teachers and systems offer their own spin—muscle testing, visualization, tapping, prayer. And those methods work. They've helped thousands shift stuck patterns. But what makes the SI Method different is that we don't stop at awareness—we go in and *move* the energy. We work with the body's own feedback system, locate the block, and then remove it through felt presence and intentional release. This isn't just mental reframing or gentle coaxing. It's a direct, somatic encounter with the energetic debris—and when the moment is right, we don't just honor it. We pull it. We clear it. We reclaim that space, not as theory, but as embodied truth.

Because the most powerful clearing tool you have is not a script or a pendulum—it's presence. It's your ability to stay with the feeling, without flinching. To recognize that beneath every block is a part of you that was doing its best. And now? It's time to let that part rest.

You don't need to understand every block's origin to begin. You just need to meet what's here now. With breath. With awareness. With willingness to feel. That's enough to open the door.

Feeling Energy: The Energy Orb Practice

Before we dive into clearing, let's pause and get present. This work begins in the body, and it begins here. You've heard the term "energy" a hundred times by now. But now? You're going to feel it.

This part may seem a little "woo" on the surface—but it's also deeply practical. You are an energetic being. Your heart produces an electromagnetic field. Your brain emits measurable frequencies.

In Eastern systems like Traditional Chinese Medicine or Ayurveda, this is called **qi** or **prana**. In modern terms, you might hear it described as **biofield energy**—the subtle electrical and magnetic currents surrounding and flowing through your body. And when something blocks that flow—trauma, repression, unprocessed emotions—the stagnant energy doesn't just vanish. It settles. It stores. It waits for a moment of release.

That's why we're starting here—with a simple, intuitive, deeply personal energy practice. One that reminds your system how to feel again. One that reawakens the part of you that knows exactly how to move energy—because it's been doing it all along.

This is the very practice I started with many moons ago when I was diving into this work on a much more intellectual level. Prior to this, I thought I was just "pretending" to have a gift to feel and clear energies. Not because I didn't believe in it or was faking it but because I was told by society that it was phony and just snake oils. When I started really looking into the world of energy, I would practice the following steps to get a better understanding of how I can create energy with my bare hands.

Step-by-Step: How to Create and Feel Your Energy Orb

Step 1: Rub your hands together.

Start by rubbing your palms briskly together for about **10–15 seconds**. Feel the warmth. The friction. Imagine you're lighting a fire in your own hands. This activates the nerve endings and begins to wake up your awareness of subtle sensation. I like to use this as a way to wake up the hands prior to doing energy work.

Step 2: Separate your hands slowly.

After you've warmed them up, gently pull your hands apart to about **6–8 inches**—the size of a grapefruit. Keep your palms facing each other.

Step 3: Begin to notice.

Pause here. Let your awareness settle between your palms. What do you feel?

Tingling?

A buzzing current?

A slight resistance, like magnetic pushback?

Warmth, coolness, or static?

This is your energy field. Subtle, yes—but real. You're not imagining this. You're perceiving it.

Take some time with this as you start out. I want you to feel the difference in the sensations from you rubbing your hands and that of holding the energy with your hands. The difference might be subtle at first but as you work with it, you will start to distinguish between the two.

Step 4: Play with the distance.

Move your hands closer together, then farther apart, as if shaping an orb of air or light. Imagine you're compressing and expanding a soft, invisible ball between your palms.

Does the sensation shift? Does the "orb" feel denser at a certain distance? Is there a moment when it feels like the space between your hands is *alive*?

Let yourself notice.

Step 5: Get curious.

After you have played with steps 1-4, you can take this even further.

Ask your body:

WHAT COLOR IS THIS ENERGY?
WHAT TEMPERATURE?
DOES IT MOVE OR PULSE?
IS IT SOLID OR VAPOROUS?

You might not "see" anything—and that's okay. Let your somatic imagination support the process. Let sensation guide you more than visuals.

Ta Da!

You've just tuned in to your own energetic field. You've made the invisible, felt. This is the foundation for the clearing work to come.

Energy orbs are more than warm-up exercises. They're a recalibration. They teach you what your energy feels like when you're present, centered, and open. And they offer your body a somatic reference point for what flow actually feels like.

This is important.

Because energy work isn't about belief—it's about experience. It doesn't matter whether you believe in chakras, meridians, or auras. What matters is that you're willing to feel. To be in your body. To engage your senses in a deeper way than usual. This is presence. This is coherence. This is how your nervous system shifts from survival mode into a state of receptivity.

The orb is also a way to build a relationship with your energy. You'll return to it again and again. In moments of stuckness. In moments of overwhelm. Before clearing. After releasing. It becomes a soft landing place—one you've built with your own hands.

I do the orb practice before every energy therapy session with a client. I have also found it to be a great way to pass the time, sort of like tossing a bounce ball at the wall over and over.

THE SCIENCE BEHIND THE SENSATION

When people say energy work is "made up," they usually mean it isn't quantifiable by traditional means. But research continues to show that the body emits measurable fields of electrical and magnetic energy. Practices like Qigong, Reiki, and even intentional touch have shown physiological benefits in studies—including lowered cortisol, improved immune response, and increased heart rate variability (a key sign of nervous system regulation).

Your body is constantly exchanging information with the world around you—electrically, chemically, and energetically. The Energy Orb is simply a conscious way to tune into that information. It's not magic. It's attention. It's coherence. It's embodiment.

Use This Orb As a Tool

When we begin pulling and releasing blocks, you'll use the same awareness you cultivated here. You'll bring this orb to specific places in the body. You'll infuse it with intention. You'll let it move. The orb becomes a tool of focus, compassion, and transformation.

And even if all this feels subtle or uncertain, keep practicing. Energy sensitivity is like strength training—you build it through repetition, presence, and trust.

You don't need to be psychic. You don't need to be perfect. You just need to be willing to feel. Your body remembers how. Let the orb remind you.

The SI Method: Energetic Clearing

Now that you've created your energy orb and anchored into your own field, we begin the clearing process.

No catchy name for this one. No branding required. Honestly, trying to slap a title on this would cheapen it. This is not a technique to market. It's not a proprietary system. It's a remembering.

You already know how to move energy. Your body has done it since before you had language. When you cried as a baby and someone held you, rocked you, soothed you—your nervous system regulated not just from the touch, but from the shared energy. When you walked into a room and felt tension in the air before anyone spoke a word—that was your energy body listening. When you touched your chest during heartache, or held your stomach in fear, or instinctively placed your hands over your womb or gut in grief or protection—that was your body trying to clear, to comfort, to shift.

We're not doing something new. We're simply doing it innately.

Start with the area of the body where you felt your block or contraction earlier. You've already located it using the SI Method. You've felt it, honored it, and surrendered its grip. Now, you release it.

Bring your hands toward that space—not forcefully, not with a "get this out of me" mindset, but with respect. You're not attacking a problem. You're listening to a signal.

Let one hand hover over the area. Let the other hand hold your energy orb, like you're carrying light. Gently move your orb hand in slow circles, sweeps, or spirals over the site of the block. You might visualize the energy dissolving, unhooking, or unraveling. You might sense warmth, tingling, even a light breeze across the skin. Some people feel emotions surface here. Others feel nothing. Both are okay. The work is happening.

You are interrupting the pattern—not by analyzing it, but by changing its field.

You can imagine that the energy you're pulling out moves into your hands, or out of your field entirely. Some people like to "throw" the energy down into the earth, imagining it composting like dead leaves. Others release it into light. I will toss it into a bowl of salt water in my sessions. Do what feels aligned. There's no wrong way. Correction...there is one wrong way. Do not and I repeat DO NOT throw, shake, or point it in the direction of another being.

This process may take a few seconds or a few minutes. Let your body lead.

And remember: this is not a one-time fix. Energy builds over time. So does clearing. Just like emotional processing, just like healing, just like brushing your teeth—this is maintenance. Hygiene. Stewardship of your field. Not perfection. There will be days when you feel a surge of release and lightness. Other days will be quiet. That's not failure—it's rhythm. This work honors cycles. Trust yours.

When you feel complete, bring both hands to your heart or belly. Close your eyes. Breathe. Let your field settle. Let your system integrate.

I often feel like someone just took my breath away when I clear energetic blockages from myself. Remember the work on my marketing blocks I discussed in Chapter 5? I used this technique to pull out and remove my procrastination and perfectionism. About 2 minutes afterwards, I started to bawl my eyes out. Not out of pain but as a huge release of childhood emotions that I had clung to for far too long. It was the internal earthquake I was needing.

How Often Should You Do This?

There's no hard rule. No spiritual stopwatch ticking behind the scenes. But here's the truth:

Blocks don't just evaporate with a single session. They're sneaky. Adaptive. They loop. Not because you're doing it wrong, and not because you're broken—but because you're human. Because you live in a relational world that echoes your old patterns. Because your nervous system doesn't shift on command; it learns through repetition, presence, and safety.

So no—this isn't a "one-and-done" experience. It's a practice. Like brushing your teeth. Like stretching your muscles. Like washing your face. You don't do it once and call it complete. You do it as an act of care. Of showing up for yourself over and over.

And more importantly: because life keeps happening. New stressors arise. Old wounds get bumped. You take risks. You expand. And each time you stretch your comfort zone, the shadow might stir. The nervous system might contract. A new layer might reveal itself. That's not regression. That's the work deepening.

So how often should you clear?

When something feels stuck. When your chest tightens for no reason. When an old pattern creeps back in. When you're preparing for a new leap—whether it's a conversation, a launch, a love, a risk. You can even clear preemptively. Daily. Weekly. Before bed. After a hard day. Before a big meeting. Before or after doing deeper work in this book.

But don't forget the other half of the equation: *integration*.

It's not enough to just release. You have to let your system recalibrate.

After you clear, give yourself space to breathe. Drink water. Walk. Journal. Stretch. Place your hands on your body and whisper gratitude. Let your nervous system register that something has shifted. Go out in nature and ground.

And track what changes—internally and externally. You may notice more calm. A lightness. A decision you'd been avoiding suddenly becomes obvious. A situation that used to trigger you now feels neutral. These are signs of integration.

The clearing opens the channel. But the integration teaches your body it's safe to stay open.

That's the real magic—not in the release, but in the receiving that follows. So clear often. Integrate intentionally. And trust your rhythm. Your system knows how to heal. You're just giving it the space to remember.

Different Blocks, Different Locations

One of the biggest myths about healing is that once you "clear a pattern," it's gone forever. In reality, the same core fear (abandonment, rejection, failure) can express itself in multiple areas of life—and live in different areas of the body.

So don't be surprised if:

YOUR BUSINESS FEARS LIVE IN YOUR SOLAR PLEXUS
YOUR RELATIONSHIP WOUNDS BUZZ IN YOUR THROAT
YOUR PARENTING ANXIETY PULSES IN YOUR LOWER BELLY

Every goal may come with a different block—and each block lives in a different place.

Keep tracking. Keep clearing. You're doing it right.

Safety + Support

This work can stir things up. You're not just thinking about change—you're inviting your body to release what it's been guarding for years. Sometimes, that's smooth. Other times, it brings discomfort to the surface fast. Old memories. Sudden tears. A lump in the throat that doesn't seem to move.

If you ever feel overwhelmed—pause. That's not failure. That's wisdom. Your system is speaking. Take a moment to regulate and ground:

PLACE ONE HAND ON YOUR HEART, THE OTHER ON YOUR BELLY. FEEL THE RISE AND FALL OF YOUR BREATH.

SIP COLD WATER—SOMETHING PHYSICAL AND TANGIBLE TO RECONNECT WITH YOUR BODY.

NAME FIVE THINGS YOU CAN SEE IN THE ROOM AROUND YOU. FEEL YOUR FEET ON THE FLOOR.

LET YOUR EYES LAND ON SOMETHING COMFORTING—NATURE, A CANDLE, A PHOTO OF SOMEONE YOU LOVE.

SPEAK GENTLY TO YOURSELF: "I AM SAFE. I CAN PAUSE. I DON'T HAVE TO DO IT ALL NOW."

And if a block feels too big to move on your own—reach out. Whether it's a coach, a therapist, an energy practitioner, or a trusted mentor, you don't have to do this alone. There is no prize for processing in isolation. Having support isn't weakness—it's wise nervous system care. It's co-regulation. It's honoring your human need for safe, attuned witnessing. Sometimes the most powerful thing you can do is say, "I need help with this part." That's not bypassing. That's capacity-building.

I myself have several people I reach out to for my own energy work to be done. I have a full team I call upon including a couple massage therapists, a chiropractor, several herbalists, a coach, a sound bowl practitioner, a Chinese Medicine practitioner, and a handful of full-on energy workers. Each has their own special way of doing things and I will ask specific ones for assistance with my own growth when needed.

So keep listening to your body. Keep honoring your pace. And remember: the goal isn't to clear everything at once. The goal is to meet yourself with honesty, compassion, and care—one breath, one layer at a time.

I like to use this analogy when people talk about wanting to clear all of their shit all at once. Think of body hair waxing. For some it is tolerable. For some it is painful even for a small section. And when we get to the bikini zone...just plain masochistic torture. When getting a waxing session, you do sections at a time. Clearing all of the your shit at one time would be like dipping your whole body into warm wax and then ripping the fabric strip off all at once. Pause for facial disgust...yep, it is truly like that. Think of the amount of skin that could also be ripped off leaving you raw, exposed, hairless. Your body and more importantly, your nervous system would not know how to handle it.

So...in the meantime, let's just stick with layer by layer. I don't want to think of people walking around like raw bloody naked mole-rats.

The Shift You'll Start to Feel

It doesn't always come with fireworks. There's no drumroll. No flashing sign that says "You did it." Most shifts aren't loud. They're subtle. Almost imperceptible—until you realize that something feels... different.

Maybe your breath has more room in it. Maybe that usual knot in your stomach doesn't show up when you open your inbox. Maybe someone triggers you, and instead of spiraling, you pause. You respond—not react.

This is the shift.

It's not a high. It's not an escape. It's a return. A softening back into your body. A loosening of the grip that the old block once held.

You might notice:

YOUR JAW ISN'T CLENCHED AS OFTEN.
THOUGHTS FEEL LESS SCRAMBLED. CREATIVITY RETURNS.
YOU SLEEP MORE DEEPLY, OR YOUR DREAMS GET LOUDER.
YOU FEEL... HERE. PRESENT. LIKE YOU CAME BACK TO YOUR-
SELF.

These are not just emotional changes—they're energetic re-alignments. Your system is recalibrating. The frequency you've been living in—tight, protective, guarded—is making room for something new. And that "new" might not be joy right away. Sometimes it's just quiet. A moment of stillness that used to scare you... now feels sacred.

Let that be enough.

In Chapter 7, we'll build from here. We'll take the space you've just created and begin to raise your emotional frequency—to move from neutrality into resonance. That's where we begin to cultivate new outcomes, new patterns, and eventually... new realities.

But for now?

Pause. Breathe. Celebrate in the most grounded way possible. You've cleared something—maybe small, maybe massive—that once held power over you. And your body, your field, your nervous system... they know it. They feel the difference.

Seven

EMOTIONAL ALCHEMY

From Density to Radiance

I hesitated writing this chapter of the book. Not because it is not important or because the science is not sound but because I don't want to confuse you with this coil back to an earlier chapter. I sat around procrastinating how I was going to say all of this to make sense and not lose you in a jumble of words. I could honestly hear the cries as I tried to fall asleep at night, "Didn't I do this already?" "If you pulled it, why do I need to go back?" "Did I miss something?" "This makes no sense at all. What a quack!" Yep, this created much stress on my nervous system. It wasn't until I was talking to a class of mine, sharing my pain, that the words started to just flow from me and it all started to connect...just like I had wanted. With clarity and humility.

151

You have come a long way from the looping thoughts and familiar sabotage. You met it in your body, named it, held it, and let it unravel. Not all at once. Not perfectly. But with presence. With honesty. With more courage than you probably gave yourself credit for. Something inside you now feels different. Maybe quieter. Maybe more spacious. The grip that once held so tightly is looser. It doesn't mean the shadow is gone—but you've changed your relationship to it. You didn't run. You stayed. That's what counts.

The work doesn't end with the clearing though. It sets the stage for what your system can now hold. Because after we release, there's an opening. And that opening invites something new. Not just intellectually—but emotionally, energetically. This chapter is about how we begin to fill that space with something aligned. Something purposeful.

This is the part of the work most people skip. They clear the block and then wonder why nothing changes. But this—this is where the momentum builds. Where the frequency begins to rise. Where we start to create from the inside out.

For much work out there, the process is linear. One straight line from point A to point B. One magic pill to mask the symptom. However, like the unalome of life, our process is also looping back. We are reaching back to our SI Method to solidify this shift. We laid the foundation in Chapter 5 and now we build this tower to the sky. Tapping back into the feelings within, we use the shifts we have made to launch us into the life we are truly wanting.

So don't rush this. Stay close. Feel your way into what's possible. Before we light this fuse, though, we need to discuss more about frequency, vibrations, and the emotions that hold them.

Figure 7.1 The Unalome

The Frequency Within

Let's talk about frequency—not the trend-chasing, watered-down, spiritual wallpaper version of it. I mean the real, measurable energy that you are made of. The frequency that moves
through every cell, every thought, every emotion, every choice.
The kind that quantum physics, neuroscience, and mysticism are
finally sitting around the same table to discuss. Not perfectly. But
the overlap is undeniable.

Everything is vibration. This is not just a poetic metaphor—it's
a fundamental property of the universe. From the beating of your
heart to the thoughts spinning in your mind to the memory of
that thing you swore you got over but still feel in your gut—it's all
frequency. And it's all affecting your field.

Dr. Joe Dispenza teaches that each of us is broadcasting a signal
24/7. Your brain sends out electrical impulses. Your heart generates a magnetic field. Together, these signals create a pattern—a
vibrational imprint—of your internal state. What you think and

feel, when paired consistently, becomes the dominant frequency you live in. And that frequency has impact. It shapes how you experience the world. It informs the world how to respond to you.

Here's where it gets complicated: most people think they can change their lives by changing their thoughts. But if your body—the emotional archive that carries every trauma, every memory, every unmet need—is still vibrating in a state of fear or unworthiness, those new thoughts never truly take root. You can say, "I am safe" all day long, but if your nervous system is still bracing for impact, you're just layering noise on top of static.

That's why all the earlier work mattered. The shadow naming. The somatic unraveling. The energetic clearing. It wasn't just to "heal"—it was to *re-tune*. Because when the static starts to fade, you can actually hear the signal underneath. The one that belongs to you. The one that was there before the survival adaptations, the patterns, the noise.

And that signal? That's the frequency we're working with now. It's not some magic wand, but the literal state your body exists in. And your state determines your choices. Your choices create your outcomes. And your outcomes build the life you live in.

This isn't about pretending to feel good or forcing gratitude when your body is locked in survival. That kind of performative positivity does more harm than good—it disconnects you from what your system is actually experiencing. From a scientific standpoint, the nervous system doesn't respond to intellectual commands; it responds to *felt safety*. In a dysregulated state—when your heart rate is elevated, your breath is shallow, your muscles are bracing—your body isn't available for joy. When we override our true feelings with forced positivity, the body doesn't register safety—it registers suppression.

EMOTIONAL FREQUENCY CHART

	Frequency	Emotional Level	Emotional State	View of Life
STRONG CREATIVE	700Hz+	Enlightenment	Inspiration	Is
	600Hz	Peace	Bliss	Perfect
	540Hz	Joy	Serenity	Complete
Negativity Dissolves	500Hz	Love	Reverence	Benign
	400Hz	Reason	Understanding	Meaningful
	350Hz	Acceptance	Forgiveness	Harmonious
	310Hz	Willingness	Optimism	Hopeful
	250Hz	Neutrality	Trust	Satisfaction
Energy Expands	200Hz	Courage	Affirmation	Feasible
Energy Contracts	175Hz	Pride	Score	Demanding
	150Hz	Anger	Hate	Antagonistic
	125Hz	Desire	Craving	Disappointing
	100Hz	Fear	Anxiety	Frightening
	75Hz	Grief	Regret	Tragic
	50Hz	Apathy	Despair	Hopeless
WEAK DISTRUCTIVE ENERGY	30Hz	Guilt	Blame	Evil
	20Hz	Shame	Humiliation	Miserable

Figure 7.2 The Emotional Frequency Chart

What the field of polyvagal theory teaches us is that you can't access higher-order emotional states like empathy, creativity, or gratitude until you move out of fight-or-flight and into what's called "ventral vagal tone"—a state of calm and connection. That shift doesn't happen through mantras. It happens through micro-adjustments in breath, posture, tone of voice, and interoceptive awareness. Abraham Hicks refers to this process as climbing the Emotional Guidance Scale. But even that isn't just a woo-woo framework—it's backed by how the brain maps and responds to emotional range. You can't leap from despair to joy in a single bound because the neural networks involved in those states are too far apart. But you can take one emotional step up. From despair to anger. From anger to frustration. From frustration to neutrality. From neutrality to openness. Each of those steps activates slightly different circuits in the brain—moving from the amygdala's panic to the prefrontal cortex's capacity for choice. That's emotional scaffolding. That's how we build resilience. Not through bypassing. Through attunement.

That climb—slow, intentional, grounded—is the path of real emotional alchemy. Because it's not driven by fantasy or delusion. It's grounded in reality. Your reality. Your body.

There's a reason this chapter comes after the clearing. You've created space. You've softened some of the grip. Now you're better equipped to hold higher states—not just for a fleeting moment, but sustainably. And let me tell you, that's a bigger deal than most people realize. The ability to *feel good*—without guilt, without sabotage, without waiting for the other shoe to drop—is one of the most radical shifts a person can make.

What you are tuning into now isn't about perfection or performance. It's about coherence. Inner alignment. The point where your nervous system, your subconscious, your heart, and your conscious mind are all speaking the same language. That's when frequency stabilizes. That's when things begin to shift—not because you forced them to, but because you became congruent enough for them to.

So this is where we begin. Not at the top of the emotional ladder, but with your feet on the first rung. With breath. With honesty. With presence. And with a nervous system that's finally ready to stop running and start receiving.

Take a moment and feel into this with me. You may already have an idea of what you are feeling within but in case you forgot to write it down (not a requirement), let's tap back into it now. We are not going to move through the process just yet. It is simply good to know where our starting point is.

Growth vs. Protection: The Biological Fork in the Road

You can't be in creation and survival at the same time. Let me say that again for the nervous system in the back—you *literally* cannot build something new from a body stuck in defense mode. It's called biology.

Dr. Bruce Lipton explains that on a cellular level, organisms are wired to toggle between two modes: growth and protection. When a cell detects a threat—whether chemical, emotional, or environmental—it contracts. It diverts all its energy to self-preservation. That means no new growth, no repair, no reproduction, no forward motion. Just defense. Now multiply that by the trillions of cells in your body, and it's not hard to see why chronic stress or unresolved trauma puts the brakes on your potential. You're not lazy. You're just living in a biology of bracing.

Your nervous system plays traffic cop in all of this. It decides whether your body is safe enough to create—or whether it needs to hunker down. When you're stuck in fight, flight, freeze, or fawn, you're not building dreams. You're surviving your own chemistry.

This is where Dr. Joe Dispenza's work deepens the conversation. He shows that elevated stress keeps the brain in high beta—an aroused state that's chaotic and rigid. In high beta, the brain is constantly scanning for danger. It can't innovate. It can't imagine. It can't collaborate with the body. It loops. It obsesses. It reacts.

Most people hang out here everyday. With all of the noise in our society/culture; from television to smart phones to fast moving daily schedules to deadlines to keeping up with the Joneses this is where people set up camp in the nervous system. Constantly pegged out. Then, with any little speck of stress, they have a complete meltdown, act irrational, and show their shadow self to the world. For many, chronic stress becomes so normalized people stop recognizing it altogether. It's not that they're calm—it's that dysregulation has become their baseline. "I operate my best when under pressure." (Cough, BULLSHIT!) Sorry. Someone had to call it out.

And yes it takes one to know one. I was there for many years until it almost killed me. My body was operating at full octane. I loved the fast-paced life, the drama, the puzzles of helping others. I was doing all the things and thought I was fine. I was working in a management role, doing yoga, meditating some, and training 3 days a week in Muay Thai. On the weekends, I would be riding horses, spending time in nature, hanging with friends, and working at my family's campground. I loved my life. But I was tired for no reason...like all of the time. I started to fall asleep on my way to work in the mornings and then again on my way home in the evenings, despite all of the caffeine I had chugged throughout the day. There had been several times I woke up just in time to correct my jeep from plowing into a bluff or tumbling down a steep hill. My body was in fight or flight mode for so long that it manifested a wild case of chronic adrenal fatigue with a side of irritable bowel syndrome.

My life was truly in danger and my body was constantly trying to protect itself. And even though I was doing all of these amazing, life expanding things, I couldn't grow with them as I was stuck in protection mode.

But here's the good news: when you regulate—through breath, awareness, grounding—your brain starts shifting into alpha and eventually theta states. These slower frequencies allow for coherence between the brain and heart. They open the door to creativity, healing, and what Dispenza calls "the quantum field"—a space of infinite possibility. This isn't magic. This is the biology of receptivity.

Yep, you can absolutely meditate your way into coherence—but it's not about candles and crossed legs. It's about creating consistent, embodied cues that tell your body: *you're safe now.* Safety is not a one-time event, but a practice—a recalibration of the nervous system's default setting.

This also explains why trying to manifest from a place of panic rarely works. Your field is scrambled. You're trying to receive insight or abundance from a bandwidth your body can't even tune into. You're listening for 90s alternative and grunge while your internal radio is full of static.

True creation begins when your body stops bracing. When it no longer feels like the world is out to get you, your biology opens up. Your energy becomes less about defense and more about direction. And that's when momentum builds—not through hustle, but through harmony.

So if you've ever felt like you couldn't make progress because you "weren't trying hard enough," let that story die here. You're not broken. Your nervous system has just been doing its job too well. The shift into growth doesn't come from force. It comes from trust. From choosing, moment by moment, to teach your body that it's safe to feel good again.

Because once the body believes it's safe, everything else becomes possible.

You Can't Fake a Frequency (And You Shouldn't Try To)

Let's go ahead and cut straight through the spiritual fluff—because this section isn't going to cater to feel-good memes or surface-level affirmations. There is no shortcut to authenticity. There is no affirmation strong enough to override a body stuck in fear. And there is no bypassing the residue of trauma just by "thinking positively."

You can't fake a frequency. And honestly? You shouldn't try to.

The nervous system is a master lie detector. Like we just discussed, you might convince your conscious mind that you're "fine," but your body knows the truth. It knows when you're saying "I'm abundant" with clenched fists and a pit in your stomach, thinking about all of the bills that you need to pay. It knows when you're performing hope but vibrating shame. And it will not align with a script it doesn't believe.

This is where Carolyn Elliott's *Existential Kink* brings in a brutally honest layer of liberation. The idea that transformation isn't just about healing the pain—but about *owning the pleasure* we secretly get from it. Yes, you read that right. Pleasure. From pain.

Now stay with me.

It sounds twisted (and it is a bit) but if you've ever found yourself repeating the same toxic pattern and wondering, "Why the hell do I keep doing this?"—there's a good chance some part of you is hooked into the payoff. Maybe the drama gives you a rush. Maybe being the martyr gets you love. Maybe playing small feels safer than failing big. That's the subconscious payoff. And it's running the show.

We're not saying you deserve the pain. We're saying that part of your identity may be unconsciously woven into it.

Elliott calls this shadow pleasure—when we unconsciously get something we *like* out of our sabotage. And the only way to truly dissolve its grip is to stop pretending it's not there. To stop saying, "I don't know why this keeps happening," and start asking, "What part of me might actually enjoy this?"

That question isn't self-blame. It's self-awareness. It's the beginning of taking back your power.

Because if part of you enjoys being the fixer, the victim, the underdog, the hot mess—then pretending otherwise won't help. But *owning it?* Feeling the thrill, the charge, the pleasure of it fully? That's when the spell breaks. That's when it loses its power over you. Because you're no longer rejecting it—you're integrating it.

And that, right there, is emotional alchemy.

It's not about transcending the shadow. It's about loving it into wholeness.

You're not trying to *stop* being the version of you that created chaos. You're trying to *understand* her. To hold her. To say, "I see why you did what you did. I get the appeal. And I'm choosing something different now—not because I hate you, but because I've outgrown the game."

This process demands honesty. Real, uncomfortable, unfiltered honesty. It demands you stop trying to "vibe high" your way out of a wound and instead sit in the dark with it long enough to hear what it wants to tell you.

The moment you stop resisting your shadow—when you drop the shame and let yourself feel the hidden satisfaction, even for a moment—you're no longer its puppet. You become its witness. And from that place, you can make choices that aren't dictated by unconscious loops.

So when I say you can't fake a frequency, I don't mean you're stuck where you are. I mean you have to earn the shift by being willing to *feel* your way through. Not glossing over. Not reframing too early. Not pretending.

Frequency work isn't cosmetic. It's not a "fake it till you make it" deal. It's about resonance. Alignment. Truth. And truth doesn't always look pretty.

Sometimes truth looks like you standing in your kitchen, admitting that part of you *likes* the chaos. That it gives you control. That it keeps you "safe". And from that raw recognition, something cracks open. Something starts to change. That's how the dense becomes light.

If you think you are having a case of deja vu, you're not. Yes, we talked about this very thing earlier but hopefully you are starting to make the connections on why we need to take this one step back. What comes next? Say it with me..."Two steps forward!"

The Climb: A Somatic Rebuild

Now it's time to rebuild—not from thought, but from sensation. From the felt intelligence of your tissues, your breath, your spine. Because real, lasting change isn't intellectual. It's embodied. It happens through repetition, regulation, and presence.

Step up to where theory becomes practice.

Abraham Hicks teaches that emotion is your compass. That the way you *feel* tells you everything about how aligned you are with what you truly desire. When you feel off, heavy, contracted—it doesn't mean you're broken. It means you're out of sync with your own signal.

Dr. Joe Dispenza pushes this further: if you want to change your reality, you must pair an *elevated emotion* with a *clear intention*. **The mind sets the destination.** The body becomes the vehicle. But the fuel—the vibration that makes the journey possible—is emotion.

So the question becomes: how do you raise your emotional frequency without bypassing your humanity? How do you invite elevated states—hope, curiosity, empowerment, joy—without pretending the hard stuff isn't also real?

You climb. Not with your willpower. With your *body*. And that climb begins with presence. With listening. With letting sensation speak louder than thought.

This is the somatic rebuild. The place where we re-pattern not just how we feel—but how we *relate to what we feel*. Where we teach the nervous system that it's safe to rise. Safe to soften. Safe to expand.

Below is a simple, potent practice I call the Frequency Ladder. It's not a one-time fix. It's a ritual—a somatic muscle you build over time. Every time you use it, you're teaching your body that it's safe to shift. That it can move emotion, not just store it. That it can choose a new frequency without betraying what's true.

THE FREQUENCY LADDER PRACTICE

1. Name the Emotion

Begin by sitting comfortably and closing your eyes. We need to get honest. No sugarcoating. No bypassing. Speak what's real: "I feel fear." "I feel I'm drowning in guilt." "This stuckness feels like rage."

Language is power. When you name an emotion, you contain it. You take it out of the abstract and ground it into your awareness. You say to your system: *I'm not afraid of what I feel. I can witness this without collapsing into it.*

2. Find It in the Body

Emotions live in the body. Not the mind. So ask yourself: *Where is this showing up?* Is it a knot in your stomach? A tightness in your jaw? A weight on your chest? Maybe it's numbness, emptiness, static. There is no wrong answer.

Just locate it. Feel it—not to fix it, but to honor it.

3. Welcome It (Existential Kink Style)

Now, here's where we get brave. Channel your inner Carolyn Elliott and whisper to yourself: "Part of me might just be getting off on this."

You don't have to *like* the feeling. You just have to be curious about it. The fear might be keeping you safe. Perhaps guilt lets you avoid conflict. Maybe the sadness feels oddly familiar—like home.

When you stop rejecting your experience and start getting curious about what it offers, even in its discomfort, you pull the unconscious into the light. You reclaim the power you unknowingly gave away. Feel the juiciness of this emotion and don't shy away. No one is looking.

4. Ask the Question

Now that you've acknowledged and honored the emotion, ask: "What would feel just a little bit better than this?" Not the best. Just better.

You don't need to leap from despair to bliss. Or from grief to tenderness. From anger to determination. From anxiety to curiosity.

Let your body tell you. Let it reach toward the next available rung.

5. Embody That Frequency

Once you've identified the new emotion, practice *being* it.

If you were safe, how would you breathe? If you felt confident, how would you stand? If you believed in your own enough-ness, how would you move through this moment? Then do that.

Even for 30 seconds. Even if it feels awkward. Especially if it feels awkward. Because that awkwardness? That's just your nervous system learning a new pattern.

Let your body *try on* the frequency. Let your breath match it. Let your voice carry it. Let your posture claim it. That's how we shift. That's how we train the nervous system not just to react—but to respond. To choose. To anchor new states of being.

And every time you do this, you reinforce a new baseline. You signal to your body: *It's safe to feel. It's safe to shift. It's safe to grow.*

6. Rinse and Repeat

Continue working on this regularly. Shoot for daily.

Quick Anchors to Raise Frequency

- Breath into the chest, slow and wide
- Say out loud: "It's safe to feel good"
- Shake your limbs
- Smile (even half-fake)
- Move your spine (twist, roll shoulders)
- Put a hand on your heart
- Hum or sigh audibly

It's not a perfect process. You'll have days where you forget the ladder even exists. But every time you remember—and climb again—you're strengthening the pathway between your current state and the future you're calling in.

Your body may not rise to the next rung immediately. That's okay. Loop back to step one. Feel what's still there. Then, gently loosen your grip on it. Let your breath shift first. Then your posture. Then your energy. Send gratitude to the emotion that anchored you—and let it know you're ready to evolve. And if you feel a moment of real joy, peace, or empowerment rise up from underneath it? Fuck yeah! Go with it. Let your nervous system explore it. If not? That's okay too. One rung is enough. Just keep climbing.

Why It Feels Weird to Feel Good

Let's be honest—feeling good isn't always comfortable.

You'd think after all the clearing, the shadow work, the energy release, and the somatic shifting that your body would be celebrating. Throwing a damn parade. And sometimes it does. But often? It hesitates. It flinches. It second-guesses.

Because feeling good, for many of us, doesn't feel "normal". It feels unfamiliar. Suspicious. Even dangerous.

If your nervous system has been wired around chaos, crisis, and contraction—then peace can feel like a threat. Calm might register as boredom. Joy might feel like exposure. Safety can feel like you're waiting for the other shoe to drop.

This is not a flaw. This is conditioning. A protective mechanism your body developed to help you survive environments where ease was unsafe, where happiness was fleeting, or where being relaxed meant you weren't prepared for impact.

Your brain is wired to seek familiarity over happiness. It's called "predictive coding"—the way your nervous system constantly compares present experience with the past to assess safety. If chaos was your baseline, your system expects chaos. Peace becomes suspicious. The amygdala—the brain's threat detector—goes on high alert not because something's wrong, but because it doesn't recognize calm as safe *yet*.

As odd as it sounds, when you start to genuinely feel better—more free, more connected, more grounded—your subconscious doesn't throw a party. It throws a flag on the play.

"UMMM...THIS DOESN'T MATCH MY BASELINE."
"THIS ISN'T HOW WE USUALLY FEEL."
"SOMETHING MUST BE WRONG."

And just like that, the sabotage creeps back in. No, you didn't fail. Your nervous system is just doing its job. It's protecting you from unfamiliar terrain—even if that terrain is joy.

Bessel van der Kolk, in *The Body Keeps the Score*, writes extensively about how trauma warps our relationship to sensation. When we've lived in prolonged stress or threat, our bodies learn to equate intensity with normalcy. So when that intensity is removed, we can feel untethered. Disoriented. Numb. Or like we're floating with no anchor.

Remember my story from above? I was operating at such a high level of stress day in and day out that it became my new norm. What was I doing during this time that was so stressful? I was the program director of a psychiatric facility with a team of about 80 individuals under me. Yep...I was the head of a mental health program when my own mental health was tanking. Scary, right? But when I started to actually do the work, it felt off. I thought I was no longer being productive or leading. The reality was that I was more productive and leading from a place of calm and wisdom, not directives and authority.

It's in that space—where the old patterns have loosened but the new ones haven't stabilized yet—that many people turn back. Back to the chaos. Back to the drama. Back to the roles they know how to play. Not because they love it. But because it's familiar. My personal favorite was...*Heal. Check! I'm all good now. Time to go back to how it "should" be done.*

There's safety in the known—even if the known is miserable. This is what Carolyn Elliott describes in *Existential Kink* as the edge of pleasure. When things start to feel good, we often can't tolerate the pleasure. It's too much. Too fast. Too vulnerable. And so we subconsciously recreate just enough friction to feel "normal" again.

Here's the kicker: that return to friction *feels like relief*. The anxiety of happiness drops, and the body returns to the chaos it understands. That's how deeply embedded our survival strategies are.

So what do we do with this? We need to *normalize* the weirdness. We've got to stop expecting joy to feel immediately expansive. Stop expecting safety to feel instantly serene. And instead, begin to meet those higher frequencies with the same curiosity and compassion we brought to our shadows.

Feeling good is a skill. A practice. A capacity you build like any other. It requires just as much nervous system work as the clearing did.

When you notice yourself shrinking away from ease or pushing away support, ask yourself:

"What about this feels unfamiliar?"
"What part of me doesn't trust this?"
"What am I afraid will happen if I let this in?"

You don't have to answer with logic. Let your body speak. Let it tremble, exhale, shiver, or soften. That's the recalibration happening in real time. That's the shift. Place a hand over your heart. Feel the beat. Let your breath settle low in your belly. You don't need to force trust—just be with the wobble. That presence is the recalibration.

There's a term in psychology called "positive disintegration"—coined by Kazimierz Dąbrowski—which refers to the internal collapse of outdated mental structures to make room for more integrated ones. And that's exactly what this part of the journey is. A disintegration of your old emotional set point. Not because something's wrong. But because you've outgrown the scaffolding.

Positive disintegration is the messy middle. The tearing down of internal structures—beliefs, behaviors, even identities—that no longer align with who you're becoming. It's grief. It's vertigo. But it's also growth. You're not spiraling. You're shedding. Your nervous system isn't malfunctioning—it's remodeling.

When people say, "It feels like everything's falling apart," this is often what they mean. But in truth? Everything's falling into place—you're just not used to the new architecture yet.

So how do we stabilize joy?

We let it be uncomfortable. We let it wobble. We let it be quiet at first. Joy doesn't always announce itself with trumpets. Sometimes it slips in like a whisper. Sometimes it feels like stillness. Like less noise. Like space where anxiety used to be.

That's why so many people miss it. They expect joy to be euphoria. Fireworks. Bliss. But often, especially in the beginning, it feels more like a soft exhale. Like a steady ground beneath your feet. Like not waking up in panic.

The more you let yourself feel good—even just 1% more at a time—the more your nervous system recalibrates. The more your subconscious gets the memo: *"Hey, we're safe here. We can stay here."* Eventually, that becomes your new baseline. You *earned* it—by staying with the discomfort long enough for your body to learn that pleasure is not a threat.

It's the moment when the chaos no longer fits, but the calm hasn't settled in fully yet. So don't freak out if feeling good feels weird. That discomfort is not failure—it's progress. It means your system is stretching, adapting, evolving. It means you're expanding your capacity for joy. That's what healing looks like. And it's yours now.

The Energy You're Broadcasting

Let's bring it all together and tie it into a pretty little bow—science and soul, sensation and signal.

Now that you've cleared the density, felt the shadow, honored the sabotage, and climbed into a new emotional atmosphere, it's time to talk about what you're actually radiating.

Dr. Joe Dispenza teaches that the heart generates the largest electromagnetic field in the body. It's not a metaphor. It's measurable. The heart's electromagnetic signature extends several feet beyond your physical body—and it changes based on what you're feeling.

When you're in a state of fear, frustration, or resentment, the heart rhythm becomes erratic and disordered. Your field weakens. Your coherence drops. But when you're breathing into elevated emotions like gratitude, appreciation, compassion, or love, your heart rhythm shifts into harmony. Your field expands. Your entire system communicates in a more organized, efficient, and empowered way.

This isn't just energetic poetry—it's physics. It's neurocardiology. It's HeartMath Institute. It's your body becoming a resonant field. A transmitter. A magnet.

Research from the HeartMath Institute shows that heart coherence isn't just about feeling good—it influences cognitive performance, hormonal balance, and even immune response. Your heart isn't just broadcasting energy; it's recalibrating your biology

When your thoughts are clear and your emotions are elevated, you are broadcasting a signal that has gravitational pull. You don't "attract" from your words or your effort. You attract from your *frequency.*

This is the deeper truth behind what many people call the **Law of Attraction**. And we need to clear something up here, because it's been oversimplified to death.

The Law of Attraction isn't a spiritual vending machine. You don't just wish hard enough or think happy thoughts and magically receive everything on your Pinterest board. What you *actually* attract—or more accurately, what you *resonate with*—is the energetic match of your dominant emotional state and subconscious beliefs.

When your energy is incongruent—when you're saying "I want love" but vibrating with abandonment wounds, or saying "I want success" while pulsing with shame—you're sending a distorted signal. And that distortion creates friction in the field. You repel what you consciously want because your unconscious frequency says, "Not safe yet."

Abraham Hicks calls the space of alignment the *Vortex.* That sweet spot where your desires and your vibration are in sync. Where you're no longer begging, proving, or controlling—but simply existing in resonance with what you've already created vibrationally. In this space, you don't force manifestation. You allow it. You hold the field open long enough for what matches it to find you.

I remember very clearly when I started to learn about this woo-woo, off-the-wall bullshit (at least at the time I thought of it as some made-up scam) many moons ago. I had just finished listening to *The Secret*, the book that ended up becoming the catalyst for all that you see within me today. At the time, I was wanting to move from my good life in small town Iowa. This was a moment in my life that I was trying to keep up with the Joneses. I wanted the big house, nice yard, cookouts in the summers, steady job, climbing the ladder, collecting gadgets and meaningless things, etc. However, something within me stirred for adventure and to do things on my own terms. I had visited Southwest Missouri on several occasions and loved the area. I would dream about living there and it was quickly becoming more than just a fly-by thought or wish. My husband and I had made the decision to give it a shot.

One day, as I was driving around the area I saw a building that read "psychiatric treatment facility". I knew, at that very moment, that I wanted to work there. Every time I would drive by I would think about working there. I had no idea what they all did in this building but I knew I was going to be working there. I would tell people, "I'm going to be working right there." This was not some psychic "knowing" I'm talking about, it was more of a daydreamy thing.

Around this same time, I started casually browsing homes for sale in the area. I wasn't hunting hard. I wasn't stressed about it. I was just...playing. Dreaming. My husband and I had taken a few weekend road trips, driving through backroads and talking about what it would be like to live down here full-time. We didn't have a map—just a vision. We'd see these rolling hills, thick woods, winding rivers, and say, "Can you imagine waking up to this every day?"

We were putting ourselves into the energy of it—without knowing that's exactly how this shit works. We didn't worry about how it would happen. We just soaked in the feeling. No spreadsheets. No manifestation rituals. Just a couple of wild hearts following the feeling of "yes." That's all it took to start broadcasting a signal that the universe could meet us in.

I would look up homes for sale, daydream about what the place would look like, how it would feel once we had moved, visualize the jobs we would have, all of the fun things. So what happened? In a matter of a few months, we had sold our home in Iowa for over the asking price, packed up and moved to SW Missouri, I got the job as the new program director of the psychiatric treatment facility, and we landed ourselves a home right smack dab in the middle of our Wishlist location. Once we settled in, we finally realized it was truly in the exact area we both commented on previously on our road trips as the village we wanted to move to (we just had not seen it from the direction we came in from).

You see, I wasn't praying for this to happen. I wasn't rubbing crystals and chanting affirmations. I wasn't obsessing over it—I was just feeling good *about* it. Thinking of it like it was already happening. And that felt easy. I would smile as I browsed online for homes, I would get bubbly when talking with others about the idea of getting the sweet job in this mysterious location. Oh, yeah, and by the way...when I applied for the job from another state, I had no idea it was a job working in the treatment facility I was driving by. I was simply applying for a program director position and it just so happened to be for the program I was daydreaming of.

I had stepped into the Vortex. Although, it would be a few more years before I knew of this term and all that it meant and was going to mean to me. At the time, I didn't know I was aligning with a frequency. I just knew it felt damn good. Looking back, I can see—I wasn't forcing the universe's hand. I was finally getting out of my own way.

> YOU DON'T HAVE TO WORK AT BEING IN THE
> VORTEX. YOU JUST HAVE TO STOP DOING THAT
> THING YOU DO THAT KEEPS YOU OUT.
> Abraham Hicks

The Vortex isn't some magical alternate universe. It's not reserved for the especially spiritual or the lucky few who wake up radiant. It's a frequency range your system can *learn* to live in. It's the emotional neighborhood where clarity, alignment, joy, and knowing reside. When I was making plans to move, I would find myself feeling clear about what I wanted, and I had happiness radiating from me. All without consciously being aware of what I was doing. I wasn't trying to be in the Vortex. I wasn't forcing myself to feel gratitude or think of things as if they were already done. It easily just happened.

So then what is the key to accessing this sweet spot they call the Vortex? *How you feel when no one's watching.*

Again, this isn't about performative healing. It's about integrity. Congruence. Alignment between your inner state and your outer signal.

And here's the nuance: it's not about maintaining a high vibe 24/7. It's about knowing how to *return* to that center. To that coherence. To that place where your nervous system is regulated, your emotions are clean, your thoughts are clear, and your body feels safe enough to open to possibility.

Think of it like tuning an instrument. If you've ever tried to play a guitar that's out of tune, you know—no matter how well you strum, the sound's going to be off. You could practice for hours, memorize the chords, and still cringe at every note. That's what trying to manifest from a dysregulated nervous system feels like.

But when you're in tune—when your emotional body is humming in a frequency of trust, when your breath is steady, when your body is grounded and your thoughts are focused—that's when your reality starts to respond. That's when synchronicities appear. That's when things fall into place. You didn't force them. Your signal showed bright enough to allow them.

This is the energetic sweet spot. The place where you're not desperate, not pushing, not grasping—but not passive either. You're clear. You're connected. You're present. You're open. That's the power of frequency.

It's also why everything we've done up to this point has mattered. You can't fake this. You can't skip the clearing and expect to land in coherence. You have to be willing to excavate, to regulate, to repattern—and *then* to hold a new signal long enough for the field to shift around you.

And yes, it can feel like a quiet place at first. It can feel like nothing's happening. But don't confuse silence with stagnation. The Vortex isn't loud. It's spacious. It's clear. It's the energetic equivalent of standing in still water and suddenly seeing the reflection.

From here, everything you've been working toward starts to take shape.

Abraham Hicks reminds us: "You never get it done. And you can never get it wrong."

There's no final arrival point. No ultimate vibration you have to maintain forever. This is a dance. A relationship. A state you return to again and again, as your capacity grows.

Staying with our guitar reference; you need to continue to tune into this frequency on a regular basis. You can be strumming along, take a pause, and realize you need to retune the strings. Something was off. Sometimes you need to do it before you play, sometimes you need to do it in the middle of the jam session.

The more you practice this—this presence, this tuning, this returning—the more your baseline changes. The more your nervous system comes to recognize the Vortex not as a vacation, but as home.

So the point isn't to force the joy. It's to create the space for it. To allow it. To hold it. To become the kind of person who can live with joy—not because you escaped the hard things, but because you learned how to feel them *and* still return to yourself. Whenever you are feeling "off" or find yourself repeating those negative thoughts in your head, take some time to try and re-align yourself towards the Vortex within.

That's the bridge. From the clearings to the callings. From the shadows to the spotlight. From contraction to creation.

Eight

Quantum Manifestation

If the last chapter created hesitancy within me, this chapter scares the holy shit out of me. If you were to tell me 20 years ago that I would be writing about quantum physics, I and everyone I knew would have laughed at you and told you that you are fucking crazy. Sure, I had dabbled in the mystical and had a basic textbook understanding of psychology, but taking in the vast knowledge of the electromagnetic field and quantum physics was not on my bingo card.

I don't want to lose you in the process, but I know that if you have been able to ride this wave with me thus far, you should be good to go. Now, if you stumbled upon this chapter without reading the earlier ones...I'm sorry and buckle in.

We are in the home stretch. You are standing at 3rd base just waiting for that fly out to right field. We are just about to put the final puzzle piece in so we can step back; admiring the whole big picture of this work we have been building and digging through. Some of the information may echo previous chapters, and that is by design. It is my hope that you are starting to see the golden thread that is woven throughout these concepts and practices. Several topics in this chapter will again ring the proverbial bell inside, linking together the puzzle pieces and solidifying them for future growth.

Let's Not Get Cute About It

Let's be honest—by now, you've cleared some shit. You've felt the sabotage in your bones, crawled your way up the emotional ladder, and tuned your inner frequency like your life depended on it. (Spoiler alert: it did.)

This next phase isn't about dreaming bigger or whispering your wishes into the universe while crossing your fingers. It's not about "thinking positive" until your jaw locks up. I have seen so many people, including family members, friends, neighbors, all do this very thing in the name of their faith. "Speak it so." and then do nothing with it. Stay in the same toxic mindset and vibrational state. It makes me think of the statement I heard numerous times in my childhood..."Wish in one hand and shit in the other and see which one fills up first". Yeah, I know this is really a crappy metaphor but it is what I hear in my head when I start to think about manifestation (even after seeing it work in my own life).

This phase of the process is about aligning your biology, energy, and actions with the version of you who already lives the life you want. It's about becoming that version now—before the world hands you the proof. Thinking of manifestation as embodiment not manifestation as performance. Not, "Let me say the affirmation ten times and hope it works." But, "Let me live the frequency. Let me feel it. Let me act from it."

Imagine the moment before a musician strikes the first note on stage. The hush. The anticipation. The stillness right before sound. That's where you are right now—standing on the edge of your next creation. But instead of strumming chords or singing into a mic, you're broadcasting energy into the quantum field. And what you play... becomes your life.

THE FIELD IS THE SOLE GOVERNING AGENCY
OF THE PARTICLE.

Albert Einstein

This chapter isn't about earning your desires or begging the universe to notice you. It's about learning to hold the signal of your future self—now. Before you see the evidence. Before anyone claps for you. Before your brain stops screaming "What the fuck are we doing?"

We're diving into the quantum mechanics of creation (yep, we're bringing the science...again), seeing the role your nervous system plays in allowing or rejecting the next version of you, and what it really means to manifest through coherence—not control. This isn't magic. But it is magnetic.

So if you're tired of forcing, fixing, or waiting for "someday," you're right on time. Let's drop into the frequency that changes everything.

The Quantum Field: The Place Where Possibility Lives

The quantum field is not a fantasy or a metaphor. It's a literal sea of electromagnetic information that surrounds and permeates every atom of your being. And while that may sound like something out of a sci-fi novel—or the multiverse of Marvel—it's rooted in some of the most groundbreaking scientific theories of our time.

Quantum physics teaches that everything is energy. I mean, every-freaking-thing. Your thoughts, your emotions, the chair you're sitting in, and the body you occupy. But what's most fascinating is how energy behaves at the subatomic level. Unlike classical physics, which deals in predictable cause-and-effect logic, quantum mechanics deals in probability. Uncertainty. Potential. At this level of reality, nothing is solid, fixed, or fully determined. Everything exists in a kind of energetic limbo—until it's influenced by observation.

This is what scientists call the *observer effect*. Until something is observed—consciously focused on, emotionally felt, or otherwise interacted with—it remains in wave form. A probability. A potential. But the moment you observe it with intention and awareness, that wave collapses into a particle. It becomes real. This is not law-of-attraction fluff. This is the backbone of quantum mechanics, and it has enormous implications for how we live and create.

Imagine your life as a branching storyline—much like the Marvel multiverse (enter Dr. Strange doing his twirling, floating thing). There isn't just one possible future. There are infinite timelines available to you. Each choice, each thought, each emotion you entertain nudges you toward one version or another. Some futures are more coherent, aligned, or joyful than others. But they all exist. They're all real. Just waiting for you to tune into them.

Dr. Joe Dispenza breaks it down like this: your heart creates the *charge* through elevated emotion—think joy, gratitude, love. Your brain creates the *direction* through focused intention—clarity, vision, belief. When those two elements work in tandem, they create a coherent electromagnetic signature that speaks directly to the field. You become a signal, not just a sponge. **You influence reality instead of reacting to it.**

The key here is coherence. When your thoughts say "abundance" but your emotions are humming in scarcity, confusion, or self-doubt, the field picks up the dominant frequency—not the words. That's the hard truth of quantum manifestation: you cannot out-affirm your vibration. You can't slap a pretty mantra on a dysregulated nervous system and expect the universe to cash it in.

This is why emotional intelligence and somatic awareness matter so damn much. They allow you to *feel* your way into the signal you want to send. Not pretend. Not force. But genuinely shift. If the field responds to the energy you *are*, not the energy you *wish* you were, then embodiment becomes the practice. Alignment becomes the compass. And nervous system regulation becomes the foundation.

You've probably already experienced glimpses of this. Think back to a time when you were in total alignment. Maybe you were traveling, or immersed in your art, or lost in laughter with someone you love. Time felt fluid. Synchronicities popped up like breadcrumbs on your path. Things just clicked. That's coherence in action. That's you living in a frequency that the field can clearly respond to.

Now imagine being able to *choose* that coherence. To cultivate it. To build your day—not by reacting to circumstances—but by broadcasting the signal of your desired future. Not from a place of desperation or scarcity, but from embodiment.

This is not about controlling outcomes. It's not about hacking the universe to get what you want. It's about stepping into your role as a co-creator. A conscious participant in the unfolding of your life. You do that by attuning your inner world—your thoughts, your emotions, your physiology—to the reality you want to experience.

Just like tuning a radio dial, you can only receive the station you're matched with. You wouldn't try to listen to classic rock by dialing into a news station. The same applies here. If you want to receive a life of fulfillment, love, or purpose, you have to match the frequency of those things—not just wish for them.

And look—we're not saying you have to walk around glowing with Zen monk energy 24/7. That's not realistic. But you *can* learn to return to coherence. To regulate your field. To shift when you notice you're spiraling or leaking energy. That's the real skill. That's quantum manifestation in practice.

In comic book terms, you're not waiting to be chosen by fate or bitten by some cosmic spider. You're choosing the timeline.

You're stepping into the version of yourself who already lives that life—and letting your field do the talking.

So no, this isn't magic. But damn, it is powerful.

That's where we're going next. Not to manifest by wishing—but by *tuning*. By broadcasting. By *becoming* the signal that your future can recognize.

Preparing for Manifestation: The Internal Prerequisite

Before we talk about calling in new realities, we have to name the elephant in the room: most people try to manifest from chaos. From the fight-or-flight. From a body that's bracing for impact while a mouth says, "I'm ready to receive."

Let's be blunt: you cannot broadcast clarity from a dysregulated nervous system.

You can't trick the quantum field. You might convince a few people on Instagram. You might even fool yourself for a minute. But energy doesn't lie. The field responds not to what you say you want—but to what your body believes is possible and safe.

So let's rewind and get this part right.

Before we create, we regulate. Before we attract, we attune. That's the unsexy truth behind every truly magnetic person you've ever encountered—they're regulated. Their nervous system isn't in a frenzy. Their emotional baseline isn't confusion or panic. It's clarity, congruence, and calm.

Regulation isn't about being zen 24/7. It's about being able to return to center. To come back to a place where your system is responsive, not reactive. Where your heart rate, breath, and internal chemistry are signaling safety—not survival.

Let's anchor that in science.

The autonomic nervous system has two primary modes: sympathetic (activation, survival) and parasympathetic (rest, repair, integration). When you're in sympathetic dominance—stressed out, overwhelmed, anxious—your system is focused on short-term survival. That's not the time your body prioritizes vision or creation. It's just trying to keep you alive.

In this state, your field is fragmented. Your thoughts loop. Your emotions spike. Your internal chemistry shifts toward cortisol and adrenaline, pulling you into a narrower range of perception. This tunnel vision makes manifestation nearly impossible—because the quantum field requires openness, curiosity, and a wide lens of possibility.

On the flip side, when you're in parasympathetic regulation—when your vagus nerve is signaling calm, your heart rhythm is coherent, and your brainwaves are in more balanced states (think alpha or theta)—you enter a space of receptivity. The mind quiets. The body opens. The field expands. That's the fertile ground for manifestation. Not just spiritual rhetoric. It's neurobiology.

Do you have that weird feeling of deja vu? Good, because if this is sounding familiar, we discussed it in Chapter 6 when talking about growth vs. protection. It's the same concept.

Dr. Joe Dispenza emphasizes that elevated emotions like gratitude, joy, and compassion signal to the body and brain that the future you desire is already happening. But if you try to access those emotions while your body is still locked in hypervigilance, your system throws an error. It won't let you reach for joy if it doesn't feel safe.

So what's the move? You don't force a high vibration. You create the conditions where it can naturally rise.

This means you regulate first:

BREATHWORK TO SLOW THE HEART RATE AND SHIFT INTO PARASYMPATHETIC TONE.

SOMATIC PRACTICES TO RELEASE TENSION AND INCREASE VAGAL TONE.

GROUNDING TECHNIQUES TO BRING YOUR AWARENESS BACK TO THE BODY.

MINDFULNESS OR MEDITATION TO STABILIZE YOUR INTERNAL ENVIRONMENT.

Think of it like clearing static from a radio signal. You're not trying to shout louder—you're removing interference so the message can come through clean.

And here's where we need to clear up another misconception: regulation doesn't mean suppression. This isn't about denying fear or bypassing grief. It's about building a wide enough container that those emotions don't flood the system. It's about making space for your full humanity without letting chaos run the show. Once you've created this internal coherence, now you can move into energetic alignment. Because now your system is ready to hold the signal—not drop it.

Don't skip this part. Most people want to just jump straight to scripting their manifestations or repeating affirmations, not realizing that the body they're speaking from is in a full-blown survival state. That's like trying to stream a 4K movie on dial-up internet. It's not going to be pretty.

If you want to be magnetic, your energy needs to be stable enough to hold the charge. That's what coherence does—it stabilizes your field. It makes you trustworthy to the quantum.

Remember: the quantum field is always listening. Not to your words, but to your vibration. If your vibration says, "I'm grounded, clear, safe, and open," the field begins to organize itself around that signal. It responds not to desperation but to resonance. So before you ask, "What do I want to call in?" ask, "Am I clear enough to receive it?" Don't try to manifest through clenched teeth. Breathe. Regulate. Create from coherence. Because the universe isn't testing you. It's matching you. And the more regulated you are, the more room there is for magic to land.

Luckily for you, we have already done much of this work in the previous chapters as we work with raising the frequency from within. We have even cleared old stagnant energy from the body allowing more room for you to expand vibrationally.

Aligning with New Realities

Manifestation isn't a cosmic Amazon order. It's not about scripting your dream life on paper and then sitting back, waiting for it to land at your door via divine delivery. It's about embodiment—becoming a vibrational match for the version of yourself who already lives the life you desire. And that alignment isn't mental—it's emotional, physiological, and energetic.

In the quantum model of reality, the field responds not to your words or your willpower, but to your electromagnetic signature. Your thoughts send the signal out, but your emotions are what draw experiences back to you. I know this may sound like conceptual fluff. However, it's grounded in measurable physics. Your heart generates a magnetic field thousands of times stronger than the brain. That field shifts depending on the emotional state you're in. When you align elevated emotion with intentional thought, you're tuning yourself to the frequency of a new reality.

Let's go back to the radio for a minute. If you're set to the frequency of 88.1 FM but trying to hear what's playing on 103.5 FM, you're going to miss the music. You won't "force" 103.5 into your experience—you have to shift your dial. But there's another layer here: the strength of the broadcast and your location relative to it. Even if you're on the right station, if your receiver is weak or you're too far from the source, you'll get static. In manifestation terms, that's what happens when your frequency is technically aligned but faint—because you only visit it in short bursts, or because fear and old patterns are still overpowering the signal. It's like driving out of range of a tower—you might catch glimpses of the song, but it keeps fading in and out. The field is neutral. It doesn't play favorites. It responds to both the clarity and the strength of your coherence, and the closer you stay to that "tower" of your desired state, the stronger and cleaner the reception.

This is the invisible trap that keeps so many people looping in the same old reality. They say, "I'm calling in love," but their nervous system is still braced for the sting of the last heartbreak. Or, "I want financial freedom," while their body is still wired to flinch at every bill—running the survival programs of scarcity and unworthiness. We covered this back in Chapter 2 when we talked about autopilot and early imprinting: by around age twelve, your core emotional operating system is already set. Those unconscious patterns run the majority of your choices—about 95% of them—without you even realizing it. So when your conscious vision butts heads with your subconscious safety map, your body will choose the map every single time. Safety first. Even if that "safety" is just a familiar cage.

This is why regulation work from Chapters 5 and 6 isn't optional—it's the on-ramp to everything else. You can't leap into a new frequency if your body thinks the leap is a threat. Safety isn't simply the absence of danger; it's the presence of trust, connection, and possibility. It's the grounded space where your breath deepens, your heart rate steadies, and your mind starts running creative rather than protective code. When your system feels that kind of safety, you unlock the higher brain functions—visioning, intuition, problem-solving—that let you not only imagine a new life, but hold the frequency of it long enough for the field to meet you there.

So what does alignment actually look like?

It looks like feeling gratitude before the money arrives. Like breathing into joy before the relationship shows up. Like standing in confidence before you're given the external validation. It's not pretending. It's pre-living. You're giving your body a new blueprint.

Psychologist Dr. Tara Brach refers to this as "future anchoring"—living now in the energy of who you're becoming, not who you've been. Neuroscience confirms that when we rehearse new emotional states (and not just thoughts), we begin to lay new neural pathways. We prime the brain and body to expect the new experience. This is neuroplasticity in action—rewiring the internal so the external can respond accordingly.

Your body doesn't actually know the difference between a vividly imagined experience and a real one. Research from Harvard's neuroscience lab shows that mental rehearsal of physical actions stimulates the same brain regions as actual performance. So when you *feel* as though something has already happened—even if it hasn't shown up physically—your system responds as if it's real.

At its core, quantum creation is about turning potential into form—collapsing the wave into the particle—by living the emotional reality now. But this isn't about holding some flawless "high vibe" all day like a spiritual Olympic sport. Real alignment is measured in patterns, not perfection. Your nervous system will still have spikes and dips—that's life. What matters is the baseline you return to and how quickly you can re-tune when the signal drifts. Coherence isn't about never wobbling; it's about knowing how to find your way back to the frequency that matches the reality you're building.

Alignment isn't passive work. You don't get there by crossing your legs, humming "om," and waiting for the universe to drop your dreams on your doorstep. It's active participation—meeting the field halfway. As Dr. Joe Dispenza often says, "When your personal reality matches your personality, you've created a new destiny." In practice, that means showing up as the version of you who already lives that reality, even on the days when it feels easier to default to old habits.

That means action still matters—but it must come from aligned being, not frantic doing. When you move from the place of already being enough, already being connected, already being supported, your actions are cleaner. Sharper. More magnetic. Less hustle, more precision.

So ask yourself:

IF I TRUSTED THIS REALITY WAS ON ITS WAY, HOW WOULD I SHOW UP TODAY?

IF I ALREADY HAD THE LOVE, THE CAREER, THE HEALTH—WHAT WOULD I FEEL? HOW WOULD I WALK? WHAT WOULD I STOP APOLOGIZING FOR?

WHAT PART OF ME STILL FEELS SAFER STAYING IN THE OLD IDENTITY?

These are not hypothetical questions. They're recalibrations. Use them as cues to shift.

And yes—this work can feel uncomfortable. You're shedding the skin of your past identity, and the in-between can feel like emotional vertigo. That's okay. That's part of it. Stay with it. Breathe through it. Ground yourself in the body. You are literally becoming someone new—and not because you're broken. Because you're remembering.

Alignment isn't a grind. It's a practice of presence. A remembering of who you are beyond your conditioning. A daily act of turning your inner dial toward the reality you're calling in—not just with your thoughts, but with your whole body.

The field will do its job. But only after you've done yours. Tune in.

Here's a common tripwire: the gap between what you say and what your body believes. People recite affirmations like mantras, trying to overwrite deeply held subconscious beliefs with shiny, surface-level statements. But the body doesn't lie. If your mouth says, "I am abundant" but your gut clenches every time you pay a bill, your true signal is lack. If you declare, "I am healthy and whole," but your nervous system is still stuck in collapse, you're not in coherence. You're in contradiction.

Affirmations that aren't rooted in embodied truth can actually backfire. According to research in psychological science (Wood et al., 2009), repeating positive self-statements can make people with low self-esteem feel worse—not better—because the statement creates a cognitive dissonance that their body doesn't believe.

Embodiment means letting your physiology catch up to your vision. It means moving, breathing, speaking, and showing up in the world as if what you want is already true. And not in a performative way—in a cellular way. This isn't "fake it till you make it." It's "feel it till it's familiar."

True embodiment is a state of inner alignment, where your thoughts, emotions, breath, posture, and actions are all playing in the same key. When your system is in coherence, the quantum field responds in kind. Your frequency becomes clear, strong, and attractive—not just metaphorically, but electromagnetically.

Let's say you want to call in love. You can't just chant "I am lovable" and expect your cells to comply. You have to *experience* love in real time—give it, receive it, let it move through your breath and your body. Soften your chest. Drop your shoulders. Meet someone's gaze without flinching. That's embodiment—your body's way of saying yes to what your mind is asking for.

Want to feel abundant? It's not about a Pinterest-perfect vision board—it's about matching your emotional state to that reality now. Pay your bills with gratitude instead of dread. Tip generously, even if it's a dollar. Notice where life is already plentiful—sunlight on your skin, laughter with a friend, the fact that you're breathing without thinking about it. You're not "earning" abundance; you're normalizing it in your system.

When the body feels safe holding something new, that's when the nervous system rewires. That's when old patterns lose their grip and new pathways start firing. As we explored back in the section on regulation, safety isn't the absence of danger—it's the presence of connection, expansion, and possibility. Embodiment creates that safety.

Dr. Joe Dispenza puts it plainly: "Your personal reality is a reflection of your personality. To create a new personal reality, you must become a new personality." In other words, change your state of being, and the life around you reorganizes to match. Affirmations can plant the seed, but embodiment is the soil, the water, the sunlight.

Carolyn Elliott calls this becoming *congruent* with your desires—not just liking the idea of your new life, but trusting yourself enough to hold it without sabotage. Because here's the hard truth: the body is the gatekeeper. Your mind can declare "I'm worthy" all day long, but if your breath is shallow, your shoulders are locked, and your gut is tight, the signal is scrambled.

Embodiment isn't pretending you've already arrived. It's rehearsing the feelings and behaviors of your future self in small, sustainable ways—until they stop feeling foreign. Until your body recognizes joy, intimacy, and power not as a performance, but as home base.

That might look like:

SPEAKING YOUR AFFIRMATION WHILE BREATHING DEEPLY AND PLANTING YOUR FEET ON SOLID GROUND.

JOURNALING ABOUT YOUR VISION RIGHT AFTER YOGA, A WALK, OR A SOMATIC RELEASE—WHEN YOUR BODY IS OPEN AND RECEPTIVE.

PRACTICING CONFIDENT POSTURE AND VOICE BEFORE THE
BIG CONVERSATION, NOT TO FAKE IT, BUT TO SUPPORT
YOUR SYSTEM IN SHOWING UP.

Your body won't always believe you at first. That's normal. As we saw in the shadow work chapters, old protective patterns are designed to keep you in the familiar—even if that familiar is suffocating. The work is in showing up anyway. In building trust with yourself, one breath at a time.

Because here's what happens when you do: your cells start to echo the new truth. Not because you chanted it into submission, but because you lived it often enough for it to become real. And that's when manifestation stops being effortful.

It stops coming from performance and starts flowing from coherence. From congruence. From embodiment.

Acting from Knowing Rather Than Hoping

Hope is a beautiful thing. It's the flicker that gets us through dark days, the whisper that maybe, just maybe, something more is possible. But in the quantum field? Hope is a weak signal.

Don't get your panties in a bunch, let me explain...when you're hoping, you're still tethered to the belief that what you want isn't here yet—and might never be. Hope often carries with it a subtle undertone of doubt, of lack, of reaching for something that feels distant. Energetically, it vibrates more like yearning than receiving. It says, "I want it, but I don't quite trust it's possible." And the quantum field? It doesn't respond to your words. It responds to your signal. Remember?

Knowing, on the other hand, is an entirely different frequency. It's rooted. Steady. Embodied. It's the kind of inner alignment that doesn't need constant reassurance, because it already *feels* the outcome in motion. Knowing doesn't beg. It doesn't barter. It doesn't grip. It simply is.

Let's break it down like this:

- **Hoping** says, "I wish I could..."

- **Knowing** says, "This is who I am."

Hoping lives in the energy of waiting. Knowing lives in the energy of being.

In neuroscience terms, this mirrors the difference between a brain caught in prediction error—expecting something and not receiving it—and a brain operating from embodied belief. When your nervous system has rehearsed a new reality enough times through imagination, embodiment, and emotional resonance, your brain begins to treat that reality as familiar—even if it hasn't physically happened yet.

Dr. Joe Dispenza talks about this in terms of mental rehearsal: when you repeatedly visualize and *feel* the experience of a desired future as if it's already real, you're installing new neural hardware that your body begins to live within. You're no longer just day-dreaming. You're becoming.

Acting from knowing looks like this:

SHOWING UP TO THE CONVERSATION ALREADY BELIEVING YOUR VOICE MATTERS.

WALKING INTO THE JOB INTERVIEW WITH THE POSTURE
OF SOMEONE WHO BELONGS THERE.
MAKING THE FINANCIAL DECISION NOT FROM DESPERA-
TION, BUT FROM ENOUGHNESS.

It doesn't mean delusion. It doesn't mean ignoring red flags or pretending everything is fine. It means trusting the signal you're sending into the field because you've felt it, rehearsed it, lived it in your body before it ever landed in your hands. This is identity-based creation, not outcome-based obsession.

James Clear, in *Atomic Habits*, emphasizes the power of identity in lasting change. He writes, "Every action you take is a vote for the type of person you wish to become." The same is true in quantum manifestation. Every emotionally congruent action—no matter how small—is a vote for your future self. Not because the action guarantees a result, but because it confirms your identity.

You're no longer doing things to "get" the thing. You're doing them because they're what your future self naturally does. It's a shift from acting for results to acting from resonance. **Hope needs proof. Knowing creates proof.** One lives on the edge of arrival. The other lives in presence.

Marvel's multiverse concept actually maps surprisingly well here. Every decision a character makes in that storyline spawns a new potential timeline. The same is true in quantum physics. Every choice you make from knowing—every time you show up in alignment with your future self—you collapse the infinite wave of potentials into a particular reality. You don't just *want* a new life. You step onto the branch where it already exists.

It's not about choreographing every step or controlling the how. It's about tuning yourself to the reality you're choosing, and letting your actions flow from that inner alignment—not from whatever's happening around you. This shift might be subtle, but it's seismic.

Let's say you want to manifest a relationship. Hoping might look like scrolling dating apps with low-grade dread, putting energy into making yourself look desirable, obsessing over every message. Knowing looks like living your life as someone who is already deeply loved. You nourish yourself. You open your heart. You move through the world with the quiet, sacred confidence of someone who knows they are worth showing up for.

Or maybe it's money. Hoping is checking your account twenty times a day and reciting affirmations with clenched teeth. Knowing is paying your bills with steadiness. It's making decisions from value, not fear. It's letting your nervous system experience what "enough" feels like, even if you're still building it.

The transition from hoping to knowing won't happen in a single moment. It's a practice. A recalibration. A muscle you tone and build. And yes, you'll wobble. That's part of it. Your mind will want proof. Your body might even flinch. Old patterns will echo from deep within. But the more you lean into that inner yes—the one that lives beneath the noise—the more magnetic you become.

Knowing is less like a megaphone and more like gravity. It doesn't shout. It pulls. It centers. It's the force that steadies your steps and reshapes the space around you. Because knowing isn't loud. It's quiet. Confident. Potent. It doesn't beg. It doesn't wait. It moves. And the field moves with it.

Creating from the New Emotional Signature

Emotion is energy in motion. You've heard it before—but let's go deeper. Every time you feel something, you're broadcasting a signal. Not just metaphorically. Measurably. Your emotions shift your biochemistry, your posture, your tone of voice, and yes, say it with me—your electromagnetic field. You are a living, breathing transmission tower.

So when you generate elevated emotions like gratitude, inspiration, love, or joy—not because something happened, but because you chose to—you shift your internal state into a frequency that shapes the field around you. That's not magical thinking. That's physics. You are tuning your system to a new emotional signature, and the field responds.

Don't get this twisted. Most people misunderstand manifestation. They think it's a reward system. "If I visualize hard enough, maybe the universe will throw me a bone." But quantum manifestation doesn't work like a teacher handing out gold stars. It's not conditional. It's responsive. The field doesn't give you what you want. It reflects who you are—specifically, what you're broadcasting emotionally and energetically.

Let's talk Dr. Joe again. He teaches that your thoughts send the signal out, but your feelings draw the experience back. When the signal is strong—when elevated emotion meets clear intention—you create coherence. Your body, mind, and field line up. And in that alignment, you collapse potential into form. But if you're waiting to feel the emotion until the thing shows up—whether it's love, money, healing, or purpose—you're trapped in Newtonian cause-and-effect. "When I get the job, I'll feel worthy." "When I lose the weight, I'll feel confident." "When they love me, I'll love myself."

That's backwards. Quantum creation says: feel worthy now. Feel confident now. Love yourself now. Let the frequency precede the evidence. Let the emotion become the cause—not the effect. This is something Abraham Hicks talks about at length.

This doesn't mean pretending. It doesn't mean faking joy when you're heartbroken or straining to feel rich while your bank account begs to differ. It means finding the smallest, most accessible version of that elevated emotion and generating it from within. A spark of appreciation. A flicker of peace. A breath of possibility.

Because here's the deal: your nervous system learns through repetition and experience. The more often you generate a new emotional signature, the more familiar it becomes. You build new neural networks. You reinforce new chemical patterns. You train your system to recognize a new baseline.

It's like tuning that dang guitar. At first, you pluck a string and it's way off. You adjust. You tune. You listen again. Bit by bit, the sound sharpens. The frequency locks in. Eventually, that new note is the one your system plays naturally.

Creating from a new emotional signature is the same. It's tuning your internal state—again and again—until it becomes your new normal. Until the old emotional patterns no longer dictate your signal.

The HeartMath Institute backs this up. Their research shows that generating coherent emotional states—like gratitude and compassion—not only increases physical health markers like immune function and hormonal balance, but also enhances intuition, decision-making, and resilience. You don't just *feel* better. You *function* better. You magnetize better.

And this isn't about toxic positivity. Oh, hell no. You're not bypassing the hard stuff. You're alchemizing it. You're choosing to create from truth—not trauma. From clarity—not chaos. You're saying, "I see the fear. I feel the pain. And still, I choose a new signal."

Let's get nerdy for a moment. In quantum mechanics, particles exist in a state of probability until they are observed. Your consistent, coherent emotional signal is that observation. It collapses the wave of potential into a particular outcome. You're not just reacting to life—you're participating in its creation.

It's a bit like Marvel's multiverse, where every version of reality exists simultaneously, and your choices determine which timeline you step into. Each elevated emotion you generate is a vote for the timeline of your choosing. You're not waiting for life to hand you a new script. You're writing it with every breath, every belief, every signal you send.

Here's an example: you want to manifest a creative career. You could wait for the dream opportunity to appear and *then* feel excited and worthy... or you could wake up tomorrow, dress like someone who values their creativity, carve out time to create, surround yourself with inspiration, and embody the energy of someone who already lives that life. That emotional frequency—the confidence, the joy, the purpose—starts pulling that reality toward you like gravity.

This is identity work at its core. You're not pretending to be someone you're not. You're becoming who you've always been—beneath the fear, the patterns, the noise. You're remembering the frequency that was yours before the world taught you to forget.

So don't wait to feel better. Don't wait to feel clear, worthy, loved, or free. Generate the feeling now. Let it flood your cells. Let it rewire your system. Let it become the signal that calls your future forward.

Because once you start creating from the new emotional signature, you're no longer chasing outcomes. You're magnetizing realities.

The Vortex and Resonance-Based Creation

Let's drop into the Vortex—not as a place to get to, but as a space to remember.

As Abraham Hicks teaches, the Vortex is not a destination you arrive at by checking off a spiritual to-do list. It's a frequency band. An energetic space where your inner state matches the reality you're calling in. It's where desire and identity stop being separate. Not because you finally earned your worth, but because you finally stopped fighting it.

Think of it like tuning into a radio station. The Vortex is already broadcasting. It doesn't need your effort—it needs your alignment. When you're in tune with it, you're no longer begging, striving, or manipulating outcomes. You're not chasing. You're not performing. You're not faking it until you make it. You're simply resonating.

Resonance is the key word here. Not willpower. Not force. Not sheer optimism. Resonance. Which means your emotional frequency matches the frequency of what you desire. You're living in the energetic neighborhood of your vision, even before it becomes visible. The literal Oxford definition is the quality in a sound of being deep, full, and reverberating. The physics definition is the reinforcement of prolongation of sound by reflection from a surface or by the synchronous vibration of a neighboring object. In these definitions, the sound is our emotional frequency.

That's when synchronicity finds you. That's when people, ideas, and opportunities show up not because you tracked them down—but because you finally stopped doing the thing that kept you out of alignment. Or as Abraham Hicks puts it: "You don't have to work at being in the Vortex. You just have to stop doing that thing you do that keeps you out."

And what is that thing?

It's gripping. It's worrying. It's doubting. It's micro-managing the how. It's outsourcing your worth to outcomes.

Let's be real—most people try to manifest with clenched fists. They call it intention, but it's anxiety in disguise. They think the Vortex is something to chase, when in fact, it's something you fall into the moment you relax the grip.

Think of the Vortex like the eye of a storm. Everything around you may be swirling—life's chaos, the unknowns, the waiting. But in the center? Stillness. Clarity. Signal. That's what you're learning to access—not by controlling the storm, but by finding your center within it.

Science, again, backs this up. When you're in a state of emotional coherence—gratitude, compassion, joy—your heart rhythm becomes ordered and harmonious. That order creates a powerful electromagnetic field that extends far beyond your body. It literally shapes the space around you.

This isn't mystical woo. It's physics. Your field becomes coherent, and the quantum field begins to respond to that coherence. This is resonance-based creation in action.

Let's borrow a metaphor from Marvel for a second. Imagine the Vortex as your access point to the timeline you actually want to live in—the one where you're aligned, connected, and on purpose. Every moment you choose coherence, you're stepping into that timeline. You're not hoping it will happen someday. You're energetically becoming the version of you who already lives there.

That's the truth of quantum manifestation: you don't attract what you perform. You attract what you are. And the Vortex is where you remember who you really are—beneath the noise, the survival patterns, and the societal scripts.

So how do you know when you're in the Vortex? You feel ease. You feel light. You stop asking, "Is it working yet?" You stop needing confirmation because the frequency itself becomes fulfilling. You don't stop desiring, but the desire isn't born of emptiness. It's born of overflow. You don't crave from a lack of having. You create from clarity.

In this space, you take action—but it's not frantic or forced. It's inspired. You're not burning yourself out trying to make something happen. You're moving from inner alignment, and your action becomes the natural extension of your signal.

Even your thoughts change in the Vortex. They're not full of "what ifs" and contingency plans. They're anchored. Grounded. Certain. You're not thinking about the life you want from a distance—you're thinking from within it.

It's like stepping into a version of you who already knows. Already trusts. Already feels the fullness of the thing before it arrives. And paradoxically, that's what calls it in. Because the field doesn't respond to your wishlist. It responds to your signal. And the Vortex is where that signal gets clean, coherent, and compelling.

Let's talk about the role of the nervous system here. You can't fake your way into resonance. If your body is in a state of threat—tight jaw, shallow breath, racing thoughts—you're not in the Vortex. You're in survival. That's why regulation matters so damn much. You need enough safety in your body to access joy. Enough nervous system flexibility to move out of protection and into possibility. That's what opens the door to resonance. So join me in a gigantic inhale and slow steady exhale. Feel that? I did.

Remember this: the Vortex isn't about perfection. It's about practice. It's about returning again and again to the frequency of your future self. You'll weeble. You'll wobble. You'll forget. You may even fall off the damn wagon. But the more you come back, the more familiar it becomes. The more it becomes home. And from that home frequency? Life starts to organize around you. Not because you forced it. Not because you proved yourself worthy. But because you finally let yourself be. That's the Vortex. That's resonance. That's creation from the inside out.

Becoming the Broadcast

In the following pages, you'll find a guided meditation to help you anchor into this emotional frequency. It's not about visualizing the dream life. It's about *feeling* the new frequency, dropping it into your body, and allowing it to imprint on your system.

Manifestation isn't just theory—it's practice. This meditation is where you take everything we've covered and drop it into your body so it becomes lived, not just learned. It's not about forcing a vision board fantasy. It's about rehearsing the new emotional signature until it feels like home. The more often you return here, the more your nervous system learns that abundance, peace, and clarity are safe to hold. This isn't magic. It's repetition. Regulation. Realignment. Each time you step into this space, you're literally training your cells to recognize a new baseline.

Start with finding a comfortable place to sit or lay down. Not so comfortable that you fall asleep but I also don't want you to be thinking about that itch, the ache in your left butt cheek, or whether you are sitting up straight with a stiff spine. Close your eyes and start with some inhales and exhales.

Notice the breath as it goes in, swirls around in your belly, and then flows out on your exhale. Become fully aware of your breath and the tension that is released with each exhalation. Gently start to deepen the breath as you let go of the fear, the barriers, the negative thoughts. Find yourself feeling safe in this space. Continuing with the breath, we are going to start holding it at the top of the inhale for several beats. Allow the pressure to build slightly in the head as you restrict the exhale for a moment. Then, slowly let out your breath. Do this several more times, tapping into the pineal gland for deeper expansion.

Become aware of the space around your body. Feeling the energy that surrounds you. Surrounds your skin. Can you feel how far away that energy rings out? Stay here in this space; finding the support that is collected here.

Call forth the image of the person you want to become. The new version of yourself you are wanting to manifest and be transformed into. Take your time as you see them fully, completely. What are they wearing? What does their environment look like? What are they doing? Who is with them? How are they standing? Look at the details of them and their life. Drink it all in.

Notice them looking at you and you looking back at them. Lock eyes and hold this sacred space of knowing, understanding, loving. In your mind's eye, close your eyes and start the shift. Opening your eyes now as your new version. Still staring back at your old self. Feel into your new self. Again with detail, soak it all in. How do they feel? What do you smell? How are you holding yourself? What are you feeling deep within? Stay with this new uplifted feeling of completion, purpose, joy, ...abundance. Look around your new environment through those eyes. Taking in every little detail. Feeling the vibration ringing through your body. Can you feel it vibrate into your physical body as you sit or lay there? Let it marinate in that space surrounding you.

Tap into the heart and smile as you give thanks for the life you have. This new, amazing life that is all around you now. Looking at things or thinking those thoughts with an embrace of gratitude for all of it. Know that this version is already in existence right now. It is yours. It is your new timeline. Your new reality. Feel your heart becoming full of radiating light from within as it pushes out from your chest and begins to broadcast outward, all around you, front and back.

Slowly, bring your awareness back to your breath. Let it anchor you here—back in your body, but not back in the old patterns of guilt, shame, or lack. Notice the smile on your face, the warmth in your chest, the steadiness in your breath. That's your nervous system memorizing a new signal. That's your body saying: *this is safe now.*

Gently wiggle your fingers and toes, not as a way of "ending," but as a way of carrying this new frequency into movement. Open your eyes when you're ready and notice how the room hasn't changed, but you have. Your signal has shifted. Your trajectory honed in.

From here, move through your day as the version of yourself you just rehearsed. Ask, *What would they do? How would they respond?* How would they carry themselves? Then live into it, breath by breath. This isn't pretending. It's coherence. It's congruence. It's embodiment.

And remember: every time you return to this practice, you're not "trying to manifest." You're reinforcing a baseline. You're reminding your body and your field who you really are—and the universe has no choice but to echo it back. For best practices, do this meditation on a daily basis. Early in the morning when you first wake up is optimum as it is a time for you to set the pace for your day ahead.

Closing: This Is the New Way

You're no longer creating from lack. You're creating from alignment. You're not chasing. You're calibrating.

This isn't just a catchy reframe—it's a biological shift. The old paradigm said grind harder, prove yourself, sacrifice joy, and earn your worth. But growth doesn't come from contortion. It comes from coherence. From allowing your nervous system, emotions, and energy to line up with who you already are.

And let's be clear—this isn't spiritual bypass. You're not ignoring your trauma or faking a high vibe when your world feels messy. This work isn't about plastering a smile over a dysregulated system. It's about nervous system mastery. Emotional fluency.

Frequency literacy. It's learning how to feel without drowning, rise without escaping, and regulate instead of react.

You've learned to tell the difference between fear and intuition. Between a trauma response and a boundary. Between ego and embodiment. That's the wisdom that lets you stop surviving and start creating.

This is quantum manifestation—not as an escape hatch, but as a return. A return to your core self. To what you're capable of receiving. To the life that's been waiting for your signal to match it.

Science backs it. You are a transmitter—your heart, your brain, your field—constantly sending and receiving. The HeartMath Institute shows that when your heart is coherent, your whole system sharpens. Hormones balance. Cognition clears. Intuition strengthens. And coherence ripples outward. It doesn't just change you—it changes the field, the people, the opportunities around you. That's not mysticism. That's mechanics.

So no, this isn't about chanting "I am abundant" and hoping for magic. It's the real work—the gritty, repetitive, body-level rewiring you've been doing. Clearing sabotage. Rewriting the script in your cells. Shifting from reaction to response. Training your system to hold a higher frequency and return to it faster each time.

That's why you're not grasping anymore—you're gravitating. You're not striving—you're resonating. And the field is listening.

Of course, echoes of the old story will still surface. They're not failures, they're residue. Don't panic. Stay in your body. Stay in the frequency. That's how you'll know you're aligned—not because everything outside is perfect yet, but because you feel different. Grounded. Clear. Alive.

Manifestation shifts when the chase ends. When performance falls away. When waiting and doubting get replaced with presence and trust. You'll feel it as a hum in your chest, an opening in your gut, a clarity in your mind. You'll know: *This is what it feels like to be in tune with myself.*

And from there, you don't just manifest—you sustain. You share. You live it.

This is the new way. Not a secret. Not a shortcut. A system reboot—mind, body, energy, and field. And it ripples beyond you. Every act of regulation, every shift in frequency, every moment of alignment contributes to the collective. It all matters.

So take a breath. Tune in. Let the field respond. And prepare to be surprised by how right it feels when it all clicks into place.

Because Chapter 9? That's where it all converges. You've done the excavation. You've done the integration. Now, we build the new operating system.

Let's finish what you started.

Nine

THE WAKE-UP WAS REAL

I just have to take a moment here to give you some of my real life bullshit. I'm not going to sit here and vent to you about all of my woes, but I do want to share with you some of the life-time blocks that can happen as you do this work.

Currently, I sit here beginning, for now, the fourth time of writing this chapter. It seems odd to me as this is the chapter that we cheer you on and we bring everything into full circle, but I am struggling. The tone continues to feel off and the words start to become more lecture or lost in conversation than I want them to. Starting in this journey to write this book, I thought that once I got done with all of the sciency stuff and all of the educational bits, that I could then just coast right into the finish line, fist pump the air and BAM! I have a book. Let me break it down to you as to what is happening in my little world.

I wrote the first draft...scrapped it almost immediately. Then on to the second version with a bit more personality. That too was falling short. And with each time I would attempt to write, I was becoming more and more frustrated...no...defeated. I have been close to dropping this idea of becoming an author. It has crossed my mind more than once through this book but I had to stop for a moment and remember the work that I have already done and written here.

So we pause and take a look at the blocks within. I start back at step one and remind myself that disruption follows decision then from there, I ask the important questions to name the sabotage. Throughout the rest of this chapter, I will take you on my own journey for this book...or say, chapter writing. Also, I want to share with you other situations that may sound similar to your own. Hold tight, press play on your lo-fi rock and 90s grunge, and let's try this again.

The Call Back

Let's rewind.

Think back to where this all started—the reason you even cracked open this book. Maybe it was the dread in your chest that wouldn't quit. The late nights staring at the ceiling, wondering, *Is this it?* The Groundhog Day loop of obligations, work, and scrolling instead of living. Or maybe it was that gut-level knowing you were meant for more—but every time you reached for it, something yanked you back.

That was your wake-up call. And let's be clear—it wasn't a gentle nudge. It was that salmon slap across the face. The kind that doesn't whisper "rise and shine." It kicks the damn door in and says, *Pay attention. Something has to change.*

In Chapter One, we named it for what it was: sabotage, conditioning, nervous system programming—the outdated operating system hijacking your life without consent. You were stuck in loops you didn't even know existed. Surviving instead of living. Reacting instead of creating.

But here you are now—pages later, work done, shadows met, nervous system rewired, frequencies tuned. The wake-up was real. You didn't just hear it—you answered the flipping call.

This call doesn't come at just any time. It usually shows up when your body and brain hit a point where business as usual becomes impossible. That dread, that agitation, that voice saying *something's gotta give?* It's not random—it's biological.

Psychologist and neuroscientist Dr. Lisa Mosconi describes this stage as a kind of **"second puberty."** Just like adolescence rewires your brain for independence, midlife rewires your brain for truth and expansion. Around forty, the chemistry of your system shifts. Researchers like Dr. Louann Brizendine, Dr. Lori Brotto, and Dr. Lisa Mosconi take a deep dive into this hormonal shift. Estrogen, progesterone, and even neurotransmitters like dopamine and serotonin stop playing nice in the background. The result? The coping strategies that kept you quiet, compliant, or "fine" suddenly short-circuit.

It's why the job that once felt tolerable suddenly feels suffocating. It's why the marriage that's "good on paper" feels dead in your bones. It's why the mask you've been wearing starts to itch like hell. Your brain is literally less tolerant of bullshit.

Dr. Mosconi calls it a developmental upgrade. I call it the universe yanking the fucking rip cord. Either way, it's the same message: **you cannot sleepwalk through this any longer.**

Yes—it feels brutal. You think you're falling apart, but what's really happening is you're breaking open. The old operating system can't hold. Your biology, your hormones, your brain chemistry—everything is conspiring to push you out of autopilot and into awareness. You're not broken. You're evolving. This so-called crisis wasn't the end—it was your system demanding an upgrade.

Take Sarah. She's 43, with two lovely kids, a husband who's not terrible. However, her marriage is not exactly setting her soul on fire anymore, and even though her job does pay the bills it feels as though she is slowly bleeding out. On the surface, she's fine. And there lies the problem. Fine had become a four-letter word.

Her mornings were clockwork: alarm at 5:15, pack lunches, drive the kids, clock into work, crank through emails, then home to make dinner, fold laundry, and finally collapse in bed. Rinse. And repeat. For years, that loop felt safe. Predictable. But lately? It felt like a chokehold.

One Tuesday, sitting under fluorescent lights with a spreadsheet glowing back at her, it happened. A thought so sharp it cut through the fog: *If I keep doing this exact thing for another twenty years, I'll die inside before my body ever gives out.* Her chest tightened. Her face flushed. It wasn't a panic attack. It wasn't depression. It was biology turning the volume all the way up.

What Sarah didn't know at that moment was that her body was literally changing. A few years back, her brain started to go through her second puberty. Neurotransmitters started to recalibrate. The dopamine hits that once made routine feel satisfying stopped landing. And now the brain begins to crave meaning, not maintenance. Autopilot—once comfortable—became unbearable.

That's why Sarah couldn't scroll it away, shop it away, or wine-night it away anymore. Her operating system had hit its expiration date. The wake-up call wasn't random. It was coded into her biology.

She went home that night, stared at herself in the bathroom mirror, and for the first time in years, she didn't recognize the woman looking back. Not because she'd lost herself—but because the part of her that was asleep had just bolted upright, ready to take the wheel.

Even though others said she was just going crazy with menopause on the horizon, she knew deep down that she was not breaking down. She didn't realize that she was just breaking open. Her biology wasn't betraying her. It was demanding an upgrade.

Now take James. Fifty-six, successful on paper, respected at work, the guy who always "has it together." He's got the house, the 401k, the fishing boat that mostly sits in the garage. He should feel proud. Instead, he feels flat.

It creeps up on him quietly. First, it's forgetting why he walked into the room. Then it's the short fuse with his teenage son. Then it's the way he stares at the ceiling at 1 a.m., wondering, *Is this all there is?*

One morning, coffee in hand, he looks out the kitchen window and sees his neighbor—fifteen years younger—loading a camper for a cross-country trip. James feels a pang so sharp it borders on grief. Not because he wants the camper. Because he realizes he hasn't wanted *anything* in years.

That's the second puberty hitting from the other side. Around the early 50s, men experience their own neurochemical shift.

Testosterone tapers. Dopamine pathways rewire. The drive to achieve and conquer—the fuel that powered his twenties and thirties—no longer gives him the same rush. His body, his brain, his entire system is demanding something different: connection, purpose, presence.

But here's the trap: men like James are rarely given language for this. Culture tells him to suck it up, to buy a faster car, or to double down at work. But biology isn't asking him to hustle harder. It's asking him to wake up.

Standing there at the kitchen window, James doesn't know the term "second puberty." He just knows the old chase feels empty. He doesn't want more trophies—he wants more truth. And in that moment of quiet panic-turned-clarity, his wake-up call rings just as loud as Sarah's.

Sarah's yearning and James's hollow stare at the kitchen window aren't coincidences. Their biology was staging an intervention of the neurological type.

That's why the wake-up call feels so brutal. It's not just circumstance; it's wiring. Biology sets the alarm, but what you do when it rings—that's where the work comes in. Some people numb out, chase distractions, double down on the grind. You already know where that road leads—loops, sabotage, autopilot. But others? They choose to actually listen. To tear off the blinders, face the shadows, and start rewriting the story.

Answering the call is different. It means stepping into the very shift this book has been building toward. You've seen the wiring. You've met the saboteur. You've cleared the blocks. Raised the frequency in the quantum field. Now it's time to live the work, not just learn it.

This is where awareness turns into a new operating system. Where survival becomes creation. Where the future you've glimpsed doesn't stay a daydream—it becomes your new baseline.

Welcome to the Shift.

The One Thing

It's one thing to wake up, to feel the dread, to see the cracks in your old life. But now comes the harder question—the one that either lights you up or scares the shit out of you: *What do you actually want?*

Not the answer you give your boss or your spouse or your mom. The real one. The one you don't even like to say out loud because once you do, you can't take it back. You can't shove it back in the drawer and pretend it's not there.

That's exactly where Sarah found herself. She wasn't looking for a shiny new husband or a lottery win. She just wanted her spark back—the feeling that she was *alive* in her own damn life instead of watching it from the sidelines. For her, it started small. A pottery class on Tuesday nights. An hour where she didn't have to be wife, mom, or employee. Just Sarah. It sounds simple, almost too small to matter. But that class cracked the door. It reminded her she could want things just because they lit her up. And from there, bigger wants started to feel possible.

James was different. His "one thing" hit him one night at the kitchen table with a stack of bills staring him down. He realized he didn't actually give a damn about the promotion he was grinding toward. What he wanted—what he was almost embarrassed to admit—was more time with his son before the kid left for college.

That was it. Not a yacht. Not a corner office. Just dinners that weren't rushed. Fishing trips that weren't postponed. A chance to show up before the window closed.

For both of them, the "one thing" wasn't about fixing everything overnight. It was about finding a crack in the wall where the light could come through. Something true enough to pull them forward when sabotage tried to drag them back.

Sarah sat on her bed that night, staring at the ceiling fan spin like it had all the answers. She'd admitted it—she wanted out of her job. But almost as soon as she whispered that truth, the voices came in hot: *You can't just quit, Sarah. What about the mortgage? What about the kids' braces? Who do you think you are, chasing something "fulfilling"?*

By morning, the practical world piled on—an email from her boss, the stack of bills on the counter, a PTO form from her kid's school. Each one was like a shove back into her box. That's how sabotage shows up—not always with fireworks, but with spreadsheets, overdue notices, and the chorus of other people's expectations.

And yet, in between the noise, her truth didn't go away. It sat there, stubborn, like a splinter under the skin: *I can't do this loop for another twenty years.*

James had his own round of shadow boxing. He'd named it—he wanted more connection, more life than just numbers on a paycheck. But saying it out loud cracked something open he couldn't tape back together. He noticed the silence at dinner with his wife, the distance with his son, the way his weekends blurred into errands instead of anything that mattered. And right behind the noticing came the gut-punch of doubt: *What if it's too late?*

What if I missed my shot? What if wanting more just makes me ungrateful?

Then came the disruptions—the late-night email from work demanding another report, his son rolling his eyes at another half-hearted attempt at conversation, a buddy joking about his "midlife crisis." Every one of them dared him to shove his longing back in the drawer.

But James couldn't unknow what he knew. That hollow ache wasn't going anywhere.

For both Sarah and James, the decision wasn't clean. It never is. You don't declare your "one thing" and ride off into the sunset. You declare it, and then the doubts and disruptions show up like vultures, circling, waiting for you to cave. That's the moment that matters—not the first spark, but whether you'll let it catch when the wind tries to blow it out.

Sarah kept showing up to that pottery class, even when the guilt didn't go away. Week after week, she heard the same old soundtrack in her head: *You're wasting time. You're not good enough. This isn't practical. Why would anyone buy your mismatched bowls and warped plates?* But if she traced that voice back, she knew where it started. She had been taught—sometimes directly, sometimes in a thousand little sideways comments—that her worth came from being a wife, a mother, the steady backbone for everyone else. Not from being Sarah. Not from her own joy.

Every time she sat at the wheel, that old belief rose up like a ghost: *Don't be selfish. Don't make it about you. Your family comes first.* But with every mug she shaped, every lopsided bowl she smoothed, she pushed back against it. One night, while free-writing, she stopped mid-sentence and scrawled, *"I don't want to just be fine. I want to be alive."* Seeing it in her own handwriting was like flipping on a light. That sentence became her anchor when the saboteur tried to drag her back under.

James started testing his cracks in smaller ways too. He made a deal with himself: one phone-free dinner a week. At first, it felt awkward. He didn't know what to talk about with his wife and son besides work and school. But as the weeks went by, something softened. His son cracked a joke. His wife brought up a dream she'd shelved years ago. And James realized connection wasn't about grand gestures—it was about being all-in, even for an hour at the kitchen table.

Still, the ceiling held. Every time James said no to a project or felt the urge to slow down, a weight clamped his chest. He could hear his father's voice, sharp as a hammer: *Be a man. Don't complain. Don't show weakness.* Growing up an only child, he'd learned early to self-soothe, to stay independent, to keep feelings under lock and key. And every time he'd risked opening up in the past, someone had let him down—or worse, walked away. The result? A saboteur with one core belief: *If you want to be safe, keep grinding. Stay strong. Don't need anyone.*

But James had started writing it down, scribbling in the margins: *This isn't me. This is fear talking. This is old wiring, not truth.* Over time, the ceiling didn't shatter in one glorious smash—it thinned, it cracked, it let the light in little by little.

The breakthroughs weren't flashy. Sarah didn't suddenly quit her job and open a pottery studio. James didn't sell the house and ride off in a camper. What shifted was quieter, but sharper: they stopped believing the ceiling was solid. They stopped mistaking the saboteur's voice for their own. And every time they scribbled another raw line of truth, every time they made one small choice for aliveness over autopilot, the ceiling splintered just a little more.

That's how it goes. It's not one giant leap—it's pressure over time. The kind that doesn't just break ceilings, but rewires the whole damn house.

The Shift: Living at the Edge of a New Baseline in the Real World

So here you are—post-wake-up, raw, tender, wide-eyed. The fog has burned off, the autopilot is exposed, and suddenly the wheel is in your hands. Sounds empowering. In practice? It feels like standing barefoot at the edge of a cliff, the ground behind you crumbling, the air in front daring you to leap. And although I am deathly afraid of heights this sensation of being on the cusp of something massive is simply exhilarating. That's the shift. It isn't clean. It isn't comfortable. It's jagged, electric, disorienting—and it's exactly where transformation happens.

Remember... your old operating system—those sabotaging loops, that survival wiring—was built for safety, not fulfillment. The nervous system's first job has always been survival. Anything unfamiliar—joy, freedom, even calm—was once coded as dangerous. That's why stepping into a new baseline feels like fumbling in the dark. Your biology is literally learning a new language.

This edge is not a one-time stop. It's a place you'll return to again and again, each time you push against the glass ceiling you thought was the "limit."

Back in Chapter Four, we named that glass ceiling—the invisible wall between who you are and who you're becoming. Here in the shift, this is where you break it. But the ceiling doesn't shatter once. It moves. Every expansion creates a new "normal," and with it, a new edge.

But this is where we stand...in a place that seems amazing and exciting. Scary and nerve racking. Confusing and liberating. The only question is what do we do with all of this now? I mean all of this work has been wonderful but how do we continue the work in the midst of "real" life? I continue to sit with this very thought.

You now know all of the juicy details on why it is important to make the shift and even how you can take that leap. What is this like when you reach into your mailbox only to receive that final notice on your electricity bill just after meditating for 20 minutes? This is real. This is tough. And this is the process.

Earlier, we discussed how the vibrational shift from a low frequency to a higher frequency is not something to be done 24/7 but something to come back to over and over. The same thing with this process. You are going to find times that you are struggling, coming from a place of lack or fear. And in those moments, we need to stop, take a breath, and recenter ourselves. Only from a place of safety will we make the growth and progress we are wanting to see in our lives. Okay...I can already hear the "yeah, but". Let's talk about this a bit more.

We have to take a page from Eckhart Tolle and be present in the moment. The Now. Let's look at this very moment in life. Are you safe? Do you have a gun to your head? Look around you. Can you find things that you can be grateful for or find joy in? When you notice that you are safe, then you can make moves to your dreams.

Here's where the rubber meets the road. It's one thing to have breakthroughs on paper, another to hold onto them when the bills stack up, your boss fires off another late-night email, or the old story sneaks back in like it owns the place. That's the test—not whether you "stay high vibe," but whether you keep showing up in the middle of the mess. No mud...no lotus.

Sarah felt this firsthand. After months of stealing away to her pottery class and scribbling raw truths in her notebook, she started sketching an idea that felt impossible a year ago: a small pottery business. At first, it was just a whisper—selling a few pieces at the farmer's market, maybe opening an Etsy shop. But every time she leaned into it, the ceiling fought back. *Who are you to run a business? You don't have time. You'll never make money at this.* And still, she kept carving out time. One night a week became two. She started testing glazes in her garage, asking a friend to help her set up an online store. The doubts didn't vanish—but they stopped running the show. Sarah's "one thing" was no longer a secret wish. It was becoming real.

James's progress was quieter, but no less powerful. His vow for presence began with phone-free dinners. Then it turned into Saturday mornings reserved for fishing trips with his son. Eventually, he stopped hiding behind the grind and told his wife the truth: *I don't just want to provide. I want to be here with you.* It wasn't a Hallmark moment—it was awkward, messy, even tense at times. But little by little, the walls he'd built came down. His family didn't just see him—they started to trust he was really showing up.

Here's the thing: neither of them was "done." They still hit walls. Sarah still heard the saboteur sneer about money. James still flinched when vulnerability felt too raw. But they were moving. They were living the shift, one choice at a time.

Sarah didn't transform overnight into a confident business owner. There were nights she wanted to chuck the clay against the wall and go back to "safe and predictable." But instead of quitting, she started catching herself in the act. When the saboteur whispered, *This is selfish*, she sat down and wrote it out, named the voice, and countered it with truth: *Creating doesn't make me less of a mom. It makes me more alive, and my kids need to see that.* That became her reset.

James stumbled plenty too. One weekend he skipped the fishing trip to crank out a project for work, and by Sunday night he was hollow again. But instead of burying it, he owned it: *I chose the grind over my family, and it felt awful. I don't want that anymore.* Saying it out loud to his son was clumsy, but it mattered. His boy didn't need perfect—he needed presence. And every time James came back, even after a stumble, the trust got stronger.

This is the real work: not just waking up, but staying awake. Not just naming the saboteur once, but noticing it again and again, and choosing differently—even if the choice is small. A notebook scribble. A phone-free dinner. Two hours in the garage shaping bowls that nobody may ever buy.

The shift isn't about never slipping. It's about refusing to stay down when you do.

I see this much like an addict looking for their next drink or fix. In recovery, we talk about slips and full-on relapses. Slips are when we may fall from our path only to get back up, dust ourselves off and keep moving forward down the road. A relapse, on the other hand, is when we slip and fall but then we lay there wallowing. Some may get back up eventually, others may find the familiar comfort of being there in the muck and stay put. When you see the bills, you get the calls, your own thoughts become intrusive, you have a choice.

For me, as I write this chapter, I found myself wanting to wallow. But at the same time, I felt like a fish flopping out of water.

I knew I needed to push forward. I took a moment though in my muck to steep. Yes, like tea. I took my moment to rest, reset, and to rediscover why I set out to do this book in the first place. I then had to look at the limited beliefs I held and find the old wiring within.

Personally, I have had a pattern of starting what I thought (and others) would be amazing projects but then when I get close to finishing, I would simply stop...never to finish. I have so many art pieces in my studio that were only about a day or two away from being completed, I have other books I've started writing, musical ventures never brought to fruition, business ideas and plans hyped up but never created. Okay...that's a lot. Anyways, I was again hitting my own glass ceiling and I needed to finally move through this one so I could grow. I did the work again. I sat with the process and named the sabotage: The Critic, The Perfectionist, and The Cynic.

Even though I had already gone through this before I started to write this book, I needed to do a tune-up to the operating system. Even brand new cars and trucks have a period of time from their first rollout that they may have recalls or manufacture updates required for a smooth and safe ride. Same thing here. I had slammed into my own glass ceiling and in order to push it, I needed to do my updates.

If You Build It....:The Art of Letting Go

What happens when the limited beliefs are met with proof that things are not all rainbows and lollipops? The endless phone calls from creditors or bill stacks left unopened on the kitchen counter.

The constant rejection from potential partners or the numbers on the scale climbing higher rather than lower. You have been doing the work and have actually made quantum meditation a routine habit in your mornings. But nothing seems to be working. You try and try, but still nothing. We then need to look at letting go.

I don't mean letting go of the dream, but more like loosening your grip on it. Sounds so enlightening, right? Look at me, I should be sitting on a mountain top meditating and guiding others on the path. (Huge eye roll here) But seriously, this is the golden ticket, Charlie. And I know that I have talked about things being difficult or hard to complete, however, this is really the biggest, toughest part of the whole thing. It really isn't part of the process in a step-by-step sense, although maybe it should be. The act of letting go or surrendering to the universe, God, source, Spirit, etc. is a special balancing act that doesn't come naturally to everyone...myself included.

Once you have done all of the work, you need to have faith that it will happen...scratch that...faith that it is happening or has happened. You've seen it in the quantum field. The things you are manifesting, the new upgrades to your life, the dreams coming true. You have felt them all, wrapping their warm cashmere joy all around you. Now, you need it to integrate into your system here on Earth.

Despite what twenty-something influencers and evangelical pop ministers say, manifestation takes time. How long? For some, days or weeks, others months or years. There is no set amount of time that you will have to wait for it to all come together. I know, mood killer. I didn't make the rules of the universe; I'm just trying to muddle through them with you. I have seen it happen in my own life within days of letting go, and then I have also had times where it took years to root in.

Surrender isn't throwing in the towel. It's science-backed, soul-backed strategy. It's loosening the death grip on outcomes so your nervous system, brain chemistry, and energy field can actually line up with what you're calling in.

In Harvard's Study on Control and Stress, psychologist Daniel Wegner's work on "ironic process theory" (aka *don't think about a white bear*) shows the harder we try to *control* thoughts or outcomes, the more tightly they grip us. Letting go isn't weakness — it's stepping out of a losing game of mental tug-of-war. Carl Jung spoke about "holding the tension of the opposites," meaning we don't force an answer but let the psyche unfold its truth. That's surrender as depth psychology. Michael Singer, author of *The Untethered Soul*, argues that surrender is the art of "relaxing the grip" on life's flow, letting energy move through instead of trying to cage it. Even Abraham Hicks calls this the "art of allowing" — not passive, but actively aligning with what you want by getting out of resistance mode.

Above, I shared that this was a balancing act though. You need to find the sweet spot between letting go, allowing the universe to show itself to you and taking action in your life. I have seen both sides of this in my own life. Some people might completely let go and just talk about it happening without doing anything in their life to help it happen. This method is about as effective as buying a lottery ticket; it can happen but more than likely you are simply making a wish in an empty sky. This may look like preaching that you are going to get a 100 acre farm but never browsing properties for sale or checking your options while you live in your one bedroom apartment. I have heard people not wanting to get bug bites and they would just simply say "there are no bugs here" and hope that at the end of their nature hike they would not have ticks crawling on them or little red bumps from mosquito bites. True story.

Remember the movie *Field of Dreams*? Kevin Costner plays this Iowa farmer, Ray, who hears a voice whisper out of nowhere: *"If you build it, he will come."* On paper, it sounds like lunacy—tearing up your cornfield to build a baseball diamond for ghosts. And sure enough, everyone around him thinks he's lost his damn mind. But here's the kicker: Ray doesn't just sit in his rocking chair, praying for ballplayers to magically appear. He grabs a shovel. He rips up acres of perfectly good corn. He builds the field. And only then do Shoeless Joe Jackson and the legends of baseball step out of the stalks.

That's surrender in action. It wasn't passive wishing—it was trust paired with sweat. Ray couldn't control who would show up, or when. But he did his part. He built the damn thing.

On the other hand, you can also hold so tightly to doing the work that you never allow it to show itself. You continue to see only the negative because you are doing the work on the negative. Never being able to open your eyes to see how things are lining out for yourself. I fall into this category. I tend to do the work over and over and over but never stop and just be in the present moment without fear. Then, I complain that it hasn't happened but I just ended up not seeing it when it did crack up. I would continue to focus on the bills on the table, the empty classes in the studio, the lonely counseling groups. Instead, I should have seen the inquiries about yoga coming in various formats, the opportunities to connect and expansion for my other business prospects. Are you sensing a theme here? I was in a state of lack, of fear, sitting in a place of protection, not open for growth or feeling the...gratitude within.

Sarah wrestled with this too. She had her pottery wheel, her late-night notebooks full of ideas and strength building truths, her tiny Etsy shop starting to stir. But the bills didn't stop arriving, and every time she logged into her bank account, the saboteur's voice got louder: *This isn't safe. You'll fail. You'll embarrass yourself.* She would grip harder—planning obsessively, reworking glaze recipes, comparing herself to other potters online until her chest was tight. The more she clutched at success, the further it seemed to slip. Her turning point came the night she sat at the wheel, clay refusing to center under her hands, tears dripping onto the mud. Instead of forcing it, she dropped her hands, closed her eyes, and whispered: "I trust it's already here." That tiny act of surrender didn't erase the bills, but it shifted the current. Her next piece came out lopsided, imperfect—and she kept it. Sold it, even. Letting go wasn't about everything looking polished. It was about creating anyway, and letting the outcome take shape in its own damn time.

James hit this in a different way. He had started the phone-free dinners, the Saturday fishing trips, even the hard talks with his wife. Progress was there, but every time a work deadline loomed, he'd feel the old weight clamp down on his chest. Provide. Produce. Don't slack. He'd tighten his schedule, double-book his calendar, and push presence to the back burner. Connection felt fragile, like it would disappear if he didn't control every variable. One night, sitting in his truck outside the house after a late meeting, he caught his reflection in the windshield—tired, hollow, fighting the same fight. He thought of his son waiting inside, and for the first time, he didn't force himself to "fix" it. He let the fear sit. He let the silence stretch. And then he walked in empty-handed—no solutions, no grand plan—and asked his kid if he wanted to watch a movie. They laughed that night. James didn't have it all figured out, but he finally loosened his grip on needing to.

For both of them, surrender didn't mean quitting. It meant loosening the white-knuckle grip on outcomes long enough for life to breathe like a fine wine. Sarah learned to let her mugs dry crooked and still put them on the table. James learned to stop orchestrating every moment and simply be in it. The bills, the doubts, the old voices didn't vanish. But the more they let go, the more the field opened space for something else: possibility, presence, even joy.

So when you find yourself in this very spot, and yes, you will be here at some point, let me shed some ideas on how you can let go just a bit more and allow the universe to unfold in front of your eyes.

MEDITATION

Even though we have talked about how doing quantum meditation over and over can stir unease and more tension if you are not also working on letting it settle, meditation can be highly beneficial in taking you back to a place of peace and calm. Instead of meditation with a purpose, practice meditation with the simple goal of coming into the body using the breath. The point of this is to remind your body and nervous system that you are safe and to find the space to grow. Simply close your eyes and bring your awareness to your breath. Trace the breath in through the nose and out the nose. Allow the mind to settle into a place of quiet.

At any time if the mind begins to run down a rabbit hole, gently guide yourself back to the breath. That's it. You can do this for one minute or ten. The idea is to again...shift.

PRACTICING GRATITUDE

Such a simple concept, but it is oh-so-powerful. The mere act of being thankful can start to show you all of the proof that things really are working out for you. Find things that you are truly grateful for. I have seen many people bypass the "truly" part and just list that standard: family, friends, etc. but think of the things that make your heart sing and warm internally. I like to say the sun shining on my face (when it is sunny out, of course). But it could be the clients that you have coming into your business. The conversations and connections you are making when you are out and about. I like to think that the smaller or more mundane the object or situation for gratitude, the more impactful in the long run. It is easy to see the bigger items, but when we start seeing the small things we refine our sights for all of the positives in our world, not just the obvious.

One phrase I heard back in the day was: **Get Not Got**. Replacing the word "got" with the word "get" changes the energy of what is being said or thought. Try it with me. "I've *got* to go get groceries." Now... "I *get* to go get groceries." The energy around the word "get" allows for a bit of gratitude to seep its way into the heart center. Try it during those times that you feel you need to do something.

CLARIFY YOUR DESIRES AND EMBRACE UNCERTAINTY

Your desires and goals are not extreme or crazy. However, maybe you are holding onto specific outcomes just a tad too strongly. You may have a specific number you are aiming for in your bank account or you are wanting to fill your courses with tons of attendees. When you don't see the specifics happening all at once, you start to drift to the world of lack again, and go back to training your vision for the negative.

Being a control freak, like me, you may find this pill a bit hard to swallow. I have a clear vision of what I want to see just about all of the time. It really is a curse at times. But when I adjust the outcomes to what truly matters, not the numbers or the dollar amount, then the grip releases. If I am concerned with the amount I am bringing into my business but it is not happening, I just need to step back and think about what really matters...the why. Why do I want to fill my studio with students or my programs with clients? It really isn't the dollars, as nice as they can be; it is about being able to connect with people and help them. Look into the why you are going down this path. Focus in on the feelings you will have once you get there. Let me say that one again...focus on the feelings.

At the same time, we need to embrace the uncertainty of how you are going to get there. Again, not easy when you are the controlling planner in your friend group (shifting my eyes side to side, counting the fingers pointing at me). My 35-step plan may not unfold in the correct order as I had the steps mapped out. The universe doesn't work that way. It is trying to connect you with your highest purpose and good.

Simplify your outcomes and the route to get there. Having your vision cluttered with multiple angles or side hustling manifestations only jams your signal to the universe because you are so scattered in your thoughts, plans, and energy. Keep it simple stupid.

TRUST IN DIVINE TIMING

Okay, I am laughing as I write this. Just keeping it real with you. I'm not laughing because it is false but because I falter here as well. Energy knows no time nor space. Time itself is an illusion. Something constructed by man not created by the universe. Why would we think that our personal timing is the same as divine timing? It really doesn't work that way. You can try to steer the universe to a specific timeline but we also need to again let go of this and have faith things will happen at the best time, when you are truly open to receive it. I gently shove you back to the above talk about fear and being safe in the present moment.

ASK AND THEN LISTEN

If you get to the point that you are needing answers or begin to think that you are speaking to no one, just ask the universe for a sign. I say universe here but I think we are all adults here and can respectfully insert God, source, Spirit, or whatever you need to use here. Seriously, just ask for a sign. It can be something wild like a watermelon when there is a foot of snow on the ground. Maybe you want to hear a specific word or song during the day. I could be vague as long as you are keeping your ears and eyes open for the signal "message received".

It is important to understand that the universe communicates differently than we may want it to. It speaks through synchronicities, meaningful coincidences that may guide you. Seeing repeating numbers, specific numbers, hearing certain sounds or phrases, having the same topic arise organically in different conversations throughout a short period of time. These are a few of the most common ways the universe may talk to you. However, like mentioned above, you can also ask for something specific for the universe to share with you to show you that it is listening and with you.

BE OF SERVICE

Nothing puts things back into perspective like serving others. Focusing on what you can give rather than what you want creates a positive energetic connection that the universe hears and responds to. Being of service can be caring for someone else in times of need by lending a friendly ear or shoulder. It can come in the form of offering your time even though your schedule is tighter than O'hare Airport on Thanksgiving weekend. It may even be the act of giving someone the last $10 you have to your name.

Acts of service takes the energy out of a place of greed for what you are wanting and instead opens you up to the universal goal of helping all. At the same time, it helps you embrace the uncertainty of life as discussed above and you let go of the urgency of your own personal gains. See what I did there? Now, you are beginning to surrender.

RIGHT NOW, IT'S LIKE THIS

One of the best phrases I have personally used to get me out of my head and into a place of ease, letting go of the control I thought I needed, is "It's like *this* now." Originally, the Buddhist phrase is

"Right now, it's like this". It comes from the Theravada teacher, Ajahn Sumedho. I have just shifted it some, but the power stays the same. Life is currently like *this*. It is neither good nor bad. It just is. The phrase itself pulls you back to the Now moment. It gives you the power to do with it what you need. It also shares that life changes constantly and the situation you are currently in is fleeting. I have used this to bring myself back to center in times where I felt the world was crumbling around me. It has grounded me in the present, and even if it is for a short time, I am reminded once again, I am safe.

Sarah had to learn this the hard way. For months she strangled her little Etsy shop with expectation, checking sales every morning like a stock ticker. Each day that nothing sold, she spiraled—convincing herself she was wasting time, selfish for even trying. But once she started weaving in gratitude—small, mundane things, like the way the clay felt cool under her hands or how her daughter asked to help her glaze a mug—something shifted. She began to notice that her shop wasn't about profit yet; it was about presence. The sales came, slowly, and not because she forced them, but because she stopped choking the process. Letting go, for her, meant celebrating each crooked cup that made it out of the kiln instead of demanding they all look perfect.

James wrestled with his own version of letting go. He still heard the old voice—*man of the house, keep grinding, don't slow down*. Every time he tried to plan the "perfect" family outing, something would fall through, and he'd feel like he'd failed. But when he softened into uncertainty—ditched the perfect plan and just asked, *What do you want to do today?*—he started to see connection grow in unplanned places. A random card game after dinner. A late-night drive with his son just to grab ice cream. His surrender wasn't stepping back from being a provider; it was loosening the grip on how connection "should" look.

Neither of them got it right all the time. Sarah still caught herself doom-scrolling other potters on social media, wondering if she'd ever measure up. James still caught himself canceling a Saturday fishing trip when the office got loud. But now, instead of spiraling, they had anchors: Sarah coming back to gratitude, James coming back to presence. That was their practice of letting go—choosing not to strangle the outcome, but to live the damn process.

Staying Awake When Life Gets Messy

Life doesn't roll out a red carpet just because you woke the hell up. Bills still pile up. Your boss still sends emails at 9:47 p.m. Kids still slam doors. That's not failure. That's life.

The work isn't about erasing the chaos. It's about staying awake inside it. Anyone can feel aligned in a yoga class or fresh out of meditation. But can you hold that thread of awareness when the noise of daily life comes crashing in? That's the real test.

Sarah leaned into it, and the shift got real. Her farmer's market table sold out one Saturday morning—every lopsided mug, every crooked bowl, gone. A local boutique asked her to do a full line for the holidays. A month later, she signed a lease on a tiny studio space, the kind with peeling paint and bad fluorescent lights, but it was hers. For the first time in decades, she woke up on a Monday not dreading the week, but buzzing to unlock that little shop and get her hands in clay. Her kids saw her lit up in a way they'd never seen before, and instead of being the mom running on fumes, she became the mom showing them what it looks like to chase a dream and make it real.

James' victories looked different, but they hit just as hard. Those Saturday fishing trips with his son? They became sacred, not negotiable. His son stopped rolling his eyes and started inviting friends along because "my dad's actually cool to hang with." His wife, who had grown used to his distracted half-presence, began to meet him with her own vulnerability—and together they started mapping out dreams they'd shelved for years. At work, James shocked everyone when he turned down a promotion. Instead of tanking his career, it lit him up—he carved out a new role with less grind and more mentorship, something that gave him purpose instead of ulcers.

These weren't fairy-tale endings. They were proof. Proof that when you stop numbing out and start living the work, the universe doesn't just pat you on the head—it meets you halfway. Sarah's newfound hobby became a business. James's strained family dinners became connection. They stopped waiting for permission and started building lives they actually wanted to be in.

That's the point. The shift isn't about waiting for a perfect moment when all the pieces line up. It's about stacking real-world victories—loud, messy, hard-won wins—until you look around and realize: holy shit, this is working.

When sabotage whispers, notice. When fear tightens, breathe. When the ceiling feels solid, push anyway.

Full Circle: That Damn Wake-Up Call

We're back where it started—the wake-up call. That gut-punch of dread, those nights staring at the ceiling, the loop of "fine" that felt like suffocation. Back then it felt like the end of the road. Now you know better. It wasn't an ending—it was a crossing.

You've seen the wiring under your patterns. You've looked the saboteur in the eye instead of blaming yourself for not being "disciplined enough." You've practiced regulation when survival mode tried to drag you under. You've learned to clear the static, to listen instead of numb, to choose instead of collapse. You've even tasted the life that's waiting—your "one thing" starting to take shape in the real world.

The wake-up call was never about burning your whole life to the ground. It was about cracking the glass ceiling inside your head—the invisible cap that dictated how much joy, truth, connection, or expansion you were allowed to touch. You've cracked it. Every time you stay awake, you shatter it a little more.

Sarah cracked it when she stopped swallowing "fine" and started letting her spark pull her toward the wheel. James cracked it when he admitted that presence mattered more than performance. They're not "done." Neither are you. This isn't about finished products—it's about refusing to sleepwalk through the time you've got left.

So here's the real work: not perfection, not pretending sabotage disappears forever. The work is staying awake when life tries to sedate you. Coming back to the map when you wander off course. Returning to the truth when the old story sneaks in.

Because the next wobble will come. The next punch in the gut, the next salmon slap across the face. And when it does, you'll know what it is. Not a breakdown. Not proof you're failing. Just another reminder to wake the hell up.

The wake-up call isn't endless. It happens once—the slap that rips you out of autopilot, the moment you can't go back. But what does keep going is the work. The echoes. The evolution. The practice of staying awake when life tempts you to crawl back into "fine."

The shift was real. The wake-up was real. And now? So are you—eyes open, wide awake, living it.

The comfort zone is a coffin. You can crawl back in, pull the lid shut, and rot in "fine." Or you can claw your way out—bloody knuckles and all—and finally breathe. That's the choice. Stay numb and circle the same dead loops. Or torch the old script and walk headfirst into the fire of your own becoming.

No one's coming to save you. This is it. You either live awake—or you don't live at all.

Wake the fuck up. The cage is open. Don't you dare crawl back in.

Ten

CODa

Hip hip! You finished the book...or did you. Just kidding. Don't worry. You really did finish the book. However, I do want to share a few additional thoughts before I let you fly out of the nest for good.

As you were reading, you may have had some questions about specific things. There were times that I mentioned certain things but never really went into too much detail about them. That was on purpose...mostly. This chapter is where I add some more confusion to the mix and also talk about something that seems to be a common issue with doing interpersonal work such as this. We are popping back into the process for a little further analysis.

The Weight We Carry: Generational Trauma

When you start peeling back your sabotage, a lot of it wasn't even yours to begin with. Yeah, you lived it, you wore it, you acted it out—but the roots? They can go deeper. Generations deep.

Science has a word for this: **epigenetics**. Researchers have found that trauma doesn't just scar a person—it can flip genetic switches that get passed down. Holocaust survivors' grandchildren show heightened stress responses. Children of war survivors and those raised in households of addiction often carry higher baseline anxiety, even if they never lived the original trauma themselves. The body remembers. The wiring remembers. And it doesn't just remember your story—it remembers theirs.

Energetically, it's the same deal. Old wounds echo through the line. The scarcity your grandmother felt during the Great Depression can show up as you hustling and doomsday prepping or never trusting there's "enough." Your father's silence, born of his own unspoken pain, might echo in you as a gagged throat every time you try to tell the truth. The pain doesn't vanish when someone dies—it lingers, like smoke in the walls of a house.

James carried this inheritance like armor he never asked for. His father was a man of duty—strong, stoic, relentless. Vulnerability wasn't an option; survival meant providing, performing, keeping emotions locked up tight. And that script didn't start with his dad. James's grandfather grew up in the Great Depression where food mattered more than feelings, and his great-grandfather came home from war with silence where words should've been. Each generation handed down the same commandment: don't feel, just endure. Grind. Provide. Stay strong.

The science explains why. Trauma adaptations wire the nervous system for protection, not presence. Studies on famine survivors in the Netherlands found metabolic and stress-response

242

changes two and three generations out. Descendants of Holocaust survivors show altered cortisol regulation decades later. Trauma teaches the body to brace, conserve, and silence expression—and those instructions get carried forward long after the danger has passed.

But genetics isn't destiny. James began to notice the cracks. When he barked at his son with the same clipped tone his father used, he recognized it as an echo from the past, not his own truth. When his chest tightened every time he tried to slow down or open up, he started writing it down: This is old wiring, not me. That noticing gave him room to choose differently.

Here's where physics offers a metaphor: resonance. Just as one vibrating string can set another humming, trauma reverberates down family lines until someone interrupts the frequency. James started doing just that. A phone-free dinner. A fishing trip he didn't cancel. A conversation where he admitted—not perfectly, not eloquently—that he wanted more than grind. Each small act shifted the frequency his family was living in.

The HeartMath Institute has shown that the heart produces an electromagnetic field measurable several feet outside the body, shaped by emotional state. Trauma makes that field jagged and incoherent. Regulation and presence smooth it into coherence, which in turn calms the nervous systems of those around you. James's calmer heart rhythms weren't just about him—they became a nervous-system cue of safety for his son and wife. Energy doesn't stop at the skin. It ripples.

Psychologist Murray Bowen called this "differentiation"—the ability to see the family pattern without being fused to it. From a quantum perspective, it's the same: when one person shifts their frequency, the whole system nudges toward a new baseline.

That's the paradox of generational trauma: it's sticky enough to echo through DNA and nervous systems, but fragile enough to be interrupted by one person saying, the cycle stops here. James' son didn't need speeches; he needed to feel his father regulate, to see him show up with open energy instead of armor. That's what began to rewrite the legacy.

When you do this work, you're not just breaking your loops—you're breaking theirs. Every time James admitted, "I don't have it all together" he wasn't just finding presence—he was undoing a century of men shackled by silence.

That's why this work matters. Clearing sabotage isn't selfish. It's generational repair. It's turning to your kids—or the next generation, blood or chosen—and saying: the cycle stops here.

Yep, you betcha. It's heavy. But it's also liberating as fuck. Because when you finally put down what was never yours to carry, you don't just stand taller—you give everyone after you permission to rise too.

Beyond Bloodlines: Ethereal Trauma

Generational trauma is one layer of inheritance—the biology, psychology, and family patterns that echo through DNA and nervous systems. But for many, that's not the whole story. Some of what we carry doesn't come from our parents or even our great-grandparents. It comes from somewhere deeper, older, harder to name. Call it soul memory. Call it karmic imprint. Call it past life echoes. Whatever the label, the idea is the same: we sometimes feel the weight of wounds we never personally lived. This is **karmic inheritance**.

Psychologists working in transpersonal fields have studied this under the umbrella of "past-life recall" and "soul trauma." Ian Stevenson at the University of Virginia famously documented children who reported memories of lives they never lived—memories later verified with uncanny accuracy. Carl Jung himself spoke of the collective unconscious as a kind of psychic reservoir where archetypal patterns and unhealed stories linger, ready to surface in the lives of those who follow.

Physics, oddly enough, gives us a metaphor for this too. Energy doesn't disappear—it transforms, carries forward, reshapes. Trauma, like energy, may not die within one lifetime; it can ripple through the field of consciousness itself, finding new expression until it's resolved.

In practice, ethereal trauma often looks like disproportionate reactions: a paralyzing fear of water without ever having nearly drowned, a throat that locks up whenever you try to speak truth even though your childhood was "safe," a gut-level terror of abandonment that feels bigger than your biography. These can be the fingerprints of old stories your soul hasn't yet finished with.

Energy psychology approaches this not with proof, but with presence. The goal isn't to verify whether you were burned at the stake in 1623 or lost in famine in another era—it's to honor the intensity of the pattern and allow it to release. Modalities like regression therapy, quantum healing, or even deep somatic work often bring these echoes into awareness, not as history lessons, but as unfinished frequencies ready to be shifted.

Here's the liberating part: whether you frame it as epigenetics, karmic inheritance, or past lives, the process of healing is the same. You notice the pattern, you ground in the present, you remind your nervous system you are safe now. That act alone interrupts centuries—or lifetimes—of repetition. I highly recommend finding a reputable energy practitioner or energy psychologist to guide you through the process if you begin to find yourself muddling through. There is nothing wrong with asking for help, especially if it is in dealing with quantum.

Because trauma, whether inherited through blood or etched into the soul, carries the same paradox: it echoes until someone stops to listen. And when you choose to listen—when you decide the cycle ends here—you're not just healing yourself. You're closing a loop that may have been spinning for generations, maybe lifetimes.

When Growth Collides with Love

One of the hardest parts of growth isn't the inner work—it's realizing that not everyone around you is growing at the same pace. You start naming sabotage, shifting your nervous system, seeing patterns more clearly...and then you look across the table at your partner and feel the gap. It can sting.

When you wake up, not everyone around you wakes up with you. You're rewiring your beliefs and your biology while your partner, family, or friends may still be running on the old operating system. That gap can feel like an earthquake under your feet. Our culture and society will reverberate the general conceptions and "appropriate" practices even if it is updated or completely in line with the rest of the sheep of the herd. I don't want this section, though, to become a soapbox rant about how we are just blindly following the "ideals" of our community. So I won't. Just note that we need to be mindful of how others are still not fully awake yet. They may not have had their own wake up call or maybe they decided to not answer the call. Let's jump back in.

Sarah lived this. As she leaned deeper into her pottery—moving from participating in Tuesday night classes, to farmer's market tables, to sketching a studio of her own—her husband didn't clap and cheer. He frowned at the bills. He muttered about "wasting time." He asked when this "hobby" would stop eating into family weekends. It wasn't cruelty—it was fear. He was still plugged into the old wiring: stability above all, predictability over possibility. To him, risk meant danger, not growth.

Psychologists call this **homeostasis**—a system's natural resistance to change. Families, marriages, even friendships all have their own glass ceilings. When one person shifts, the system fights to restore balance, even if that balance was suffocating. It's not malice—it's physics. Energy seeks equilibrium.

Developmental psychology adds another layer. Robert Kegan's research shows adults evolve through stages of meaning-making, but not on a shared timeline. One person may be cracking ceilings while another is still circling old loops, not because they're unwilling, but because their nervous system isn't at the same threshold yet.

So what do you do when your shift collides with their stuckness?

The first thing is this: don't shrink yourself to fit someone else's comfort zone. It might feel easier in the short term, but silencing yourself for the sake of keeping the peace corrodes intimacy. Resentment will build even without you fully being aware of it. Little by little, you will begin to resent your friend or partner...creating further distance between you. Research shows authenticity—even when disruptive—creates stronger long-term bonds than hiding your truth. You can't stay awake and keep pretending to be asleep at the same time.

The second thing is how you communicate. Turning your growth into a sermon will only make someone defensive. But sharing from your own experience—curiosity instead of criticism, vulnerability instead of control—creates a safer space for both of you. It sounds more like, *"Here's what I've been noticing in myself"* than, *"Here's what you should be doing."* That difference matters, not just psychologically but physiologically—because it keeps both nervous systems from flaring up in defense. I like to keep these conversations short and sweet. You don't want to continually state how wonderful life is for you now and how you are doing X, Y, and Z through manifestation...yadda, yadda, yadda. Wait for them. Let your nuggets of awesomeness allure them like whiffs of coffee on an autumn morning. When they are ready, they will come to you and then you can dive deeper into the juicy details of all that you are doing.

And finally, there's patience. But patience isn't passivity. Boundaries matter. You can love someone at their pace without shrinking back into sabotage yourself. It's a balancing act: honoring their threshold while still honoring your own. Their nervous system may still crave the old loops of safety while yours is reaching for expansion. That doesn't make either of you bad or wrong—it makes you human.

At the beginning of the book, I shared how disruption follows decision and how we need to be prepared for the many different forms this can come in. One way the disruption will hit is through the disapproval of the work you are about to do. Your loved ones could be the thing that will derail your whole progress and may even nail you down in your current place.

In my own marriage, I have communicated what I was doing and what I was wanting to accomplish, but I never go much further than that. After twenty years of marriage, I know that my husband, as well-meaning as he is, will squash my chi. So, I have to practice the above mentioned suggestions. There are days that I don't talk about what I am doing in my business or in my creative projects. Other nights, we sit on the couch and we spiral together in this work. He lets me vent all that I have. More often, however, this is closer to the end of special projects or inner work that I am doing, so I can keep the momentum going.

The physics of this mirrors quantum entanglement—two particles influencing each other even at a distance. You can't shift your frequency without it rippling into the field around you. Sometimes the other person rises to meet it. Sometimes they don't.

Sarah also learned this the hard way: she couldn't drag her husband along. She couldn't force him into excitement about her clay-covered hands and late nights at the wheel. What she could do was keep creating, keep breathing, keep living awake. And over time, he noticed—not because she convinced him, but because aliveness is hard to argue with.

Look...betraying yourself to stay in sync with someone else isn't love. It's fear dressed up as loyalty. And the whole damn point of this work has been moving out of fear and into freedom.

Rounding Out to Homeplate

Endings are rarely clean. You don't finish a book like this and suddenly stop wrestling with old wiring. Life won't care that you've turned the last page—the bills will still come, people will still test your edges, and the saboteur will still try to slip in through the cracks. But now you've got something you didn't have before: a map. A way back to yourself when the fog rolls in.

Integration isn't a grand gesture. It's the quiet, everyday practice of choosing differently. Catching yourself before you drift back into autopilot. Taking a breath before snapping. Saying yes when you mean yes, and no when you mean no. Simple moves, maybe, but they're the proof that you're no longer sleepwalking.

You won't get it right every time. None of us do. But you'll notice faster, reset quicker, and return to center with more ease than you ever could before. That's the work—not perfection, not arrival, but staying awake in a world that keeps trying to lull you back to sleep.

So here's where we land. This is the end of the book, not the end of the work. Take what you've uncovered here, carry it into your days, and keep choosing presence. Keep choosing truth. Keep choosing awake.

ACKNOWLEDGEMENTS

I wanted to take a moment to give my gratitude to the numerous individuals that helped me throughout this process and journey. Without this support, I am not sure this book would be what it is now.

Thank you to my family first and foremost. My husband, Ryan and my free-spirited daughter. You both were there in the back of my mind as I was writing, knowing this was all for you two. Thank you for not squashing my chi as I grappled with the artistic process of writing and self-doubt.

There were several people, including John B., Pamela G., Tracy L., Krista E., Hannah W., and Pam M. that were my guinea pigs... I mean early readers of the book. Thank you for being part of The Wake-Up Room and for your feedback throughout the journey. Having you read the book chapter by chapter as it was being written boosted my drive to get this finished. Below, I give several of you special shoutouts.

Elisabeth B., my editor, thank you so much for taking the time to review every line, every word, and every strange comment throughout the book. You have an amazing gift for narrowing in on the details.

To Charlotte H., you were my personal sounding board. Even though we were supposed to be doing yoga, you allowed me to be completely unfiltered and vomit my thoughts out on the studio floor. Our conversations often were the driving force behind getting over the hurdles of writer's block and to openly share what needed to be said in the most authentic ways, as if we were just sitting around bullshitting. Thank you for your continual support.

I also want to thank the gals at Hammon's Black Walnut Emporium coffee shop for providing my mind with plenty of bean juice to stay focused and a comfortable place to write without distractions of dishes or other business tasks.

And finally, a thank you to the wild, messy, and brilliant world of pop culture. To the movies, television shows, comics, and music that became both backdrop and compass through the years—your stories, rhythms, and characters have been the metaphors and inside jokes that carried me (and maybe you, too) through. A special nod goes to the 80s and 90s, the decades that shaped and scarred and molded this beautiful creature I am today. From the grunge-soaked anthems to the late-night reruns, from Marvel heroes to baseball fields cut into corn, these cultural touchstones gave me language for both grit and wonder. I'm grateful to every brilliant work of art, music, film, and television that slipped into these pages—because in one way or another, you've always been part of the conversation.

A SPECIAL NOTE FROM ME TO YOU

F irst, thank you. Thank you for purchasing, listening, skimming, or even borrowing this book. Without you, it would be nothing more than an expensive diary. Writing it has been a hell of a ride—and an honor to create something that might spark a shift in your life.

If this book gave you even a flicker of clarity, or reminded you that there's more waiting for you, then know this: the journey doesn't stop here.

I invite you to join me in the **MindShift Program**—where we take these concepts off the page and into your life. Together, we'll dive deeper, face the shadows that have been holding you back, and ignite the fire that propels you forward. You'll have me not just as your coach, but as your fierce cheerleader and guide, walking with you as you leap into the life you've been craving.

Because reading about transformation is one thing. **Living it**—that's where the magic happens.

—Erin C. Corman, MS

References

Bowen, Murray. *Family Therapy in Clinical Practice*. New York: Jason Aronson, 1978.

Brach, Tara. *Radical Acceptance: Embracing Your Life with the Heart of a Buddha*. New York: Bantam, 2003.

Brizendine, Louann. *The Female Brain*. Morgan Road Books, 2006.

Brizendine, Louann. *The Upgrade: How the Female Brain Gets Stronger and Better in Midlife and Beyond*. New York: Harmony Books, 2022.

Brotto, Lori A. *Better Sex Through Mindfulness: How Women Can Cultivate Desire*. Vancouver: Greystone Books, 2018.

Byrne, Rhonda. *The Secret*. New York: Atria Books, 2006.

Clear, James. *Atomic Habits: An Easy & Proven Way to Build Good Habits & Break Bad Ones*. New York: Avery, 2018.

Dąbrowski, Kazimierz. *Positive Disintegration*. Boston: Little, Brown, 1964.

Dispenza, Joe. *Becoming Supernatural: How Common People Are Doing the Uncommon*. Hay House, 2017.

Einstein, Albert. Attributed quotation: "The field is the sole governing agency of the particle." Cited in Bruce H. Lipton, *The Biology of Belief: Unleashing the Power of Consciousness, Matter & Miracles*. Carlsbad, CA: Hay House, 2005.

Elliott, Carolyn. *Existential Kink: Unmask Your Shadow and Embrace Your Power*. Sounds True, 2020.

Gendlin, Eugene T. *Focusing*. New York: Bantam Books, 1981.

Hendricks, Gay. *The Big Leap: Conquer Your Hidden Fear and Take Life to the Next Level*. HarperOne, 2009.

Hicks, Esther, and Jerry Hicks. *Ask and It Is Given: Learning to Manifest Your Desires*. Carlsbad, CA: Hay House, 2004.

Hicks, Esther, and Jerry Hicks. *The Law of Attraction: The Basics of the Teachings of Abraham*. Hay House, 2006.

Heijmans, Bastiaan T., et al. "Persistent Epigenetic Differences Associated with Prenatal Exposure to Famine in Humans." *Proceedings of the National Academy of Sciences* 105, no. 44 (2008): 17046–17049.

Jung, C. G. *The Archetypes and the Collective Unconscious*. 2nd ed. Collected Works of C. G. Jung, vol. 9, pt. 1. Princeton, NJ: Princeton University Press, 1968.

Jung, Carl G. *Psychological Aspects of the Persona*. In *Two Essays on Analytical Psychology*. Collected Works of C.G. Jung, Vol. 7. Princeton: Princeton University Press, 1966.

Jung, Carl G. *Psychology and Alchemy*. Collected Works of C.G. Jung, Vol. 12. Princeton: Princeton University Press, 1980.

Katie, Byron. *Loving What Is: Four Questions That Can Change Your Life*. Harmony Books, 2002.

Kegan, Robert. *In Over Our Heads: The Mental Demands of Modern Life*. Cambridge, MA: Harvard University Press, 1994.

Lipton, Bruce H. *The Biology of Belief: Unleashing the Power of Consciousness, Matter & Miracles*. Hay House, 2005.

McCraty, Rollin, and Doc Childre. "Coherence: Bridging Personal, Social, and Global Health." *Alternative Therapies in Health and Medicine* 16, no. 4 (2010): 10–24.

Mosconi, Lisa. *The XX Brain: The Groundbreaking Science Empowering Women to Maximize Cognitive Health and Prevent Alzheimer's Disease*. New York: Avery, 2020.

Nelson, Bradley. *The Emotion Code: How to Release Your Trapped Emotions for Abundant Health, Love, and Happiness*. St. George, UT: Wellness Unmasked Publishing, 2007.

Pelz, Mindy. "Second Puberty and Midlife Brain Shifts." *The Resetter Podcast*. January 2023. https://theresetterpodcast.com/episode/second-puberty.

Potter, Jennie. *Self-Sabotage No More: How to Recognize and Remove the Hidden Blocks Keeping You Stuck*. True Potential Publishing, 2021.

Ruskan, John. *Emotional Clearing: An East/West Guide to Releasing Negative Emotions and Awakening Your Full Potential*. Hansa Publications, 1994.

Sumedho, Ajahn. *The Sound of Silence: The Selected Teachings of Ajahn Sumedho*. Boston: Wisdom Publications, 2007.

Singer, Michael A. *The Untethered Soul: The Journey Beyond Yourself*. Oakland, CA: New Harbinger Publications, 2007.

Stevenson, Ian. *Twenty Cases Suggestive of Reincarnation*. 2nd ed. Charlottesville: University of Virginia Press, 1974.

Tobi, Elmar W., et al. "DNA Methylation Signatures Link Prenatal Famine Exposure to Growth and Metabolism." *Nature Communications* 5 (2014): 5592.

Tolle, Eckhart. *The Power of Now: A Guide to Spiritual Enlightenment.* Novato, CA: New World Library, 1999.

van der Kolk, Bessel. *The Body Keeps the Score: Brain, Mind, and Body in the Healing of Trauma.* Viking, 2014.

Wegner, Daniel M. "Ironic Processes of Mental Control." *Psychological Review* 101, no. 1 (1994): 34–52.

Wegner, Daniel M., David J. Schneider, Samuel R. Carter III, and Teri L. White. "Paradoxical Effects of Thought Suppression." *Journal of Personality and Social Psychology* 53, no. 1 (1987): 5–13.

Wood, Joanne V., W.Q. Elaine Perunovic, and John W. Lee. "Positive Self-Statements: Power for Some, Peril for Others." *Psychological Science* 20, no. 7 (2009): 860–866. https://doi.org/10.1111/j.1467-9280.2009.02370.x

Yehuda, Rachel, et al. "Holocaust Exposure Induced Intergenerational Effects on FKBP5 Methylation." *Biological Psychiatry* 80, no. 5 (2016): 372–380.